There's a Great Day Coming

There's a Great Day Coming

William J. Allen

To order additional copies of this book, contact:
Xlibris Corporation
1-888-795-4274
www.Xlibris.com
Orders@Xlibris.com
65100

CONTENTS

PREFACE

W ho needs another book on the "End Times"? We are already flooded with them. So, what makes this one different, and worth reading? Good question.

My purpose for this book is not just to provide another scenario for the intriguing questions about the future. Nor is it my purpose to write a sensationalized drama of the Book of the Revelation. It is not intended to portray this or that person as the "Anti-Christ", or this or that nation as the key player in the unfolding scene.

My purpose is to demonstrate that a study of the "End Times" is best done by examining the entire Bible, for God has an overarching plan that includes the End Times, but is far more than that. Indeed, I do not believe the End Times can properly be understood apart from a thoroughgoing awareness of God's plan, revealed from Genesis to Revelation.

Failure to view Revelation or the End Times in this manner tends to result in unbalanced and sometimes inane, foolish expositions. Seeking to use the prophetic Word in fragmentary fashion makes for either incomplete or erroneous interpretations.

If one would study Revelation, one must first understand the Book of Daniel, for instance. But, in order to properly understand Daniel, one must know the history of Israel and God's plans for it. To do that requires understanding the other books of the Old Testament.

Still, that would not properly deal with the subject, for the Gospels and Epistles of the New Testament are filled with information necessary to round out our study of the End Times. We need to understand the nature and scope of the Church and its relation to Israel.

In other words, we must carefully uncover and delve into each part of the Bible, if we are to properly understand what God's future plans involve. For the Bible is a coherent, cohesive whole—a revelation of God's plan and purpose. To handle such an important subject in a fragmentary fashion is to invite misunderstanding and confusion.

That is why you will find that many subjects peripheral to or even mere background for the End Times study are included here. I want us to have a full-orbed view of the End Times. For I believe that a major problem with much of the Church's Bible studies today is that we persistently fragment the Bible, examining it in bits and pieces, never seeing the whole. This is often true in our books, our Bible classes, and our Sunday sermons. The result is too many Christians who may know something about bits and pieces of the Bible, but who are functionally illiterate about how it all fits together.

Throughout my teaching ministry, I've sought to teach through the various books of the Bible, providing context, background, and historical and geographical and chronological information, rather than handling them in disjointed fashion. My objective has been to make sure those listening know the entire Bible, not just certain portions.

Why should I write on this very interesting, but chancy subject? After all, we are dealing with the future, and God does not provide every piece. Well, I'm no genius, and I have no unique insight, but I do bring many years of preparation and study to the table.

I've been a Pastor-Teacher for more than 35 years, in four different churches, in three states (Connecticut, Texas, and New York). I was the founder of my current church ministry and have been serving this independent, Bible Church for over 26 years. I've taught courses on the End Times a dozen or more times, in this church and everywhere I've been.

My travels have been fairly broad, including extended trips to Israel, Greece, and Turkey. I organized and led two groups of our people to Israel and to Turkey.

My theological education includes a ThM (cert) from Dallas Theological Seminary, with a major in Systematic Theology, four years of Biblical Greek, and two years of Biblical Hebrew. In addition, I have studied Latin, French, and German intensively, along with World and American History, among other disciplines.

In this work, you won't see the "Anti-Christ" identified. You won't learn about the involvement of Iran, Iraq, North Korea, Russia, or any other nation.

You won't hear that Middle East oil is the lubricant that explains the End Times.

But you will find a solid understanding of the End Times and the events leading up to them, including:

- An exposition of Daniel 9:24-27.
- An exposition of Matthew 24 and 25.
- An in-depth consideration of the "Day of the Lord".
- A thorough analysis of the concept of "Dispensations" in the Bible.
- A comprehensive view of the "Kingdom of Heaven".

These and many other items will help you acquire a better-rounded understanding of the End Times. To buttress this, I've included Scripture references, for you to study on your own.

I would encourage you to read this book carefully. Then, with Bible and notebook in hand, read it again, more deliberately, taking the time to look at each Bible reference. I'm confident that, if you will do that, you will gain much more than a fresh look at the End Times.

So, let's begin—enjoy.

Bill Allen
Connecticut, 2009

CHAPTER 1

A Look Ahead

Israel in the end days will be alive, and yet a bit unwell. The Israelites will be living in the land, but, as is true today, will be in a threatened and somewhat uncomfortable status; surrounded by enemies and desperately needing allies.

Israel will be a sovereign nation, but anxious for powerful friends. The world will be in a fretful, tentative condition or frame of mind, anxious for some assurance of peace and stability. World events will have reached a serious, confusing, and threatening condition.

Wars, famines, pestilences, earthquakes, and weather disturbances will be increasing at an exponential rate. Christianity will have been experiencing overt and vicious opposition by governments and other religions. Only those elements of Christendom which have abandoned any notion of exclusivity in Jesus Christ, seeking fellowship and accommodation with non-Christian religions, are exempt from this terrifying pressure **[Matthew 24:6-8]**.

On top of all this, just recently, large numbers of "fundamentalist" and "evangelical" Christians, among others, have seemed to disappear. Many of the churches still continue, and people still warm the pews, but the loss is too great to dismiss casually. Those who are missing seem to have been definitely committed to Jesus Christ, according to friends **[1 Thessalonians 4:13-18]**.

Some of those remaining might classify themselves as "Christians". They attended these churches because of the warmth, good lifestyles and wholesome entertainment. But they did not take seriously the claims of the necessity of a personal relationship with Jesus Christ and of a new birth. After all, their parents before them were 'Christian', weren't they? These people may have been born into Christianity. Perhaps they paid lip service to the tenets and principles of the Christian faith, but did not take belief in the need for a personal relationship with Christ seriously.

But, how can one account for those missing? What could this mean? This surely could not be the "rapture" many of these folks talked and taught about, could it? This would be unthinkable, for it would mean that those who remain were not Christians after all! There must be a sensible, plausible answer.

Shortly, one arises with comforting and reasonable explanations for these strange events. He is a major leader of the European and English-speaking world community **[Daniel 7:7-8]**. He has recently made giant strides to impose his leadership on all the others, having pushed aside three other major leaders of this community. His appearance, demeanor, apparent wisdom and political skill all contribute to a broad acceptance of his leadership **[2 Thessalonians 2:8-12; Daniel 9:26b; Daniel 7:8; Daniel 11:36-37]**.

This man provides a number of plausible explanations for the upsurge in natural disasters. He blames them on "global warming", "proliferating population" and similar arguments easy to see and grasp. He calls for strong community-wide controls, to be administered by a benevolent but strong central leadership. He himself is the clear choice to spearhead these tightened controls and edicts **[Daniel 7:8]**.

Some suggest that he is growing too powerful; that he is seizing all power for himself. Others rebut this with the argument that such centralization of power is essential in the increasingly complex, difficult and confusing conditions the Euro-American world now faces. They thank God (or, Mother Nature) for bringing such a powerful personality to the fore in these trying times.

Still, how can even such a charismatic individual as this Great Man hope to explain the unexplainable—the massive disappearance, worldwide, of so many **[2 Thessalonians 2:10-12]**?

Such mysteries are disturbing, even if one might give a small sigh of relief at having been rid of so many gadflies and troublemakers as these "Bible toting, Bible thumping fundamentalists" and the intolerant, prejudiced "Evangelicals" **[2 Timothy 4:3-4]**. For all of these, irrespective of what church they belonged to, had insisted one must have belief and trust in the person and work of Jesus Christ in order to be acceptable to God the Creator. They insisted that Christ was the only way. They were unwilling to accept the equality of other religious views.

The news media begin to endorse and analyze approvingly the Great Man and his explanations and programs. While his suggestions might not cover every circumstance and situation, on the whole they seem to make sense.

Perhaps these missing "fanatics" have gone into hiding, foolishly awaiting the "return of their savior". Maybe they committed mass suicide, *a la* the Jones sect. Possibly a remnant surreptitiously disposed of the bodies in lakes, seas, and obscure places.

Whatever the reason, the inescapable result is evident. The world can now freely get on with the business of saving itself from over-population, global warming problems, and political and social conundrums, without the sniping of these narrow-minded individuals. They were a great deal of trouble and contributed little toward resolving these vital issues.

Having cemented his power among the Euro-American community, the Great Man focuses on centralizing his authority and arranging for a common currency. He organizes a region wide unified 'defense force' (with himself as commander-in-chief). Calling a community-wide Congress, the Great Man now determines to finally settle the simmering, troublesome Middle Eastern problem.

He travels to Jerusalem and boldly declares that he, personally, will be the protector of Israel's peace and security. Any person or country who threatens them will be answerable to the Great Man and his powerful "defense force" **[Daniel 9:27a]**.

Offering an olive branch to the Arab world, he nonetheless declares that the security of Israel is non-negotiable and he will not tolerate a continuance of animosity towards this tiny state. This is a bold and courageous initiative to undertake, and the Israelis are delirious with joy. For the first time since the days of Solomon, they are truly free of fear of their neighbors.

He has obtained agreement from the Muslims to permit a small part of the Temple Mount to be available to Jews for resumption of sacrifices. However, they would never be able to build an actual temple there.

Here is a man with a strong hand at the helm of world affairs. He is just what has long been needed. He does not deal in compromises and political shenanigans. He decides what the right thing to do is and dares to do it. He has so consolidated his power that none dare oppose him. True, Russia remains a force, as does China and India, but none of these is prepared to oppose the Great Man or the covenant he makes with Israel.

The popularity of the Great Man now increases exponentially throughout his domain and with Israel. He is seen as truly the pathfinder, the leader, indeed a savior of the world. Although the natural disasters continue, and famine still rears its ugly head, the Great Man has answers. In time, he will undoubtedly solve all these problems. After all, they were generations in the making. One ought not to expect overnight cures.

Never has the Euro-American world seen such peace and tranquility, both politically and socially. All the various religious bodies are beginning to reconcile their differences and are moving toward an ecumenical, centralized church of all faiths. This "big tent" religious group is finally bringing peace to a world weary with centuries of sectarian fighting. The religious leaders are also at peace with the non-religious thinkers in the world. There's room for everybody. The important thing is to get along and to respect one another's beliefs (or, non-belief).

A highly-respected religious figure is working to merge the Protestant and Roman Churches, and including even Jews and Muslims under the banner of this mighty secular prince. This religious leader unceasingly promotes the power, wisdom, and divine characteristics of the secular Prince, to a point of virtual worship.

Finally, the world is on track to a wonderful future, ushering in an era of peace and prosperity unequaled in history. Fights over abortion, civil rights, death penalties, sexual freedoms and "orientations", environmental issues, and political squabbles are about to become a thing of the past. "Tolerance" is the fashion of the day. Surely, there's a great day coming.

CHAPTER 2

"What's It All About?"

God has, from the very beginning, established a plan for this world. Gradually, through His revelations to chosen prophets and apostles, He has unveiled much of this plan in the form of Scripture. (By "Scripture", we mean the 66 books of the Old and New Testaments.) He has not revealed everything about His plan. He has revealed that which is important for man to know and understand.

The central message of Scripture is that God the Father intends to wrap up all of creation on this earth in the Lord Jesus Christ, His eternal Son. The Lord Jesus Christ is to be King, Judge, Savior and High Priest for man. Ultimately, all will bow the knee and recognize the supreme authority of Jesus Christ as Lord [**Philippians 2:9-11**].

However, not all men will be saved from their sins, received in holiness and acceptance with God the Father. Only those who have trusted in the Lord Jesus Christ as Savior will be saved. Christ died for the sins of the entire world, but this atonement is effective only for those who accept Him as Savior. Because Christ is God the Son, He is Infinite. Therefore, His sacrificial death is not limited, but is sufficient to cover all the sins of the entire world.

Of course, the saints of the Old Testament days did not know Jesus, the Christ, but they were accepted by God based on their belief in God [**Genesis 15:6**]; God acted in anticipating the birth and sacrificial death of His Son as full payment for their sins.

All must rely on Him and His finished work of atonement, rather than their own actions, deeds, or thoughts. Many will or would prefer to stand before their Creator for judgment, based on their own works. They will be permitted to do so, although trusting in Christ's work is the only way they can receive cleansing and be made fit for heaven. They will find at the Great White Throne judgment [**Revelation 20:11-13**]) that their works will not be sufficient to make them acceptable in a perfect heaven. The standard for heaven is *perfect* purity. They will ultimately be cast into hell—separated forever from their Creator.

Our primary purpose is to trace the plan of God, as He has revealed it in Scripture, laying it out in a reasonable and logical format. This will demonstrate that God's plan is complete and clear, and that all Scripture fits together. It is not a fragmented aggregation of books, but a cohesive whole, generated under the direction of the Sovereign God.

As God planned to focus on His Son, He began with the creation of humanity, made in the image of God. The idea was that humans would ultimately be a gift of the Father to His Son. In this way the Son would be glorified. God gradually narrowed the focus to one man, Abraham, and traced His plan through him [**Genesis 12:2; 15:4**].

Though Abraham had more than one son, God narrowed His plan for providing a Savior to Isaac [**Genesis 21:12**]. Although Isaac had more than one son, God further narrowed matters to one son, Jacob (later renamed Israel) [**Genesis 28:13-14**]. God narrowed His plan further to one of Jacob's sons, Judah [**Genesis 49:10**]. From Judah, He chose David [**1 Samuel 16:12-23**]; from David, Solomon [**Matthew 1:6**]. From Solomon, ultimately, the Christ came, as King. Christ was born of Mary's line [**Luke 3:23-38**], but His kingly authority came through the line of his "technical" father, Joseph [**Matthew 1:1-17**].

Gradually, God's plan for mankind and salvation in Christ was revealed, with the final revelation coming in the New Testament. God used several men and methods to gradually unveil His plan and to prepare men for it.

For example, God provided a series of Covenants. Although our Reformed or Covenantal friends like to insist on only two basic covenants—the Old Covenant and the New Covenant (or, the Covenant of Works and the Covenant of Grace)—there really are other important covenants which God made with man. It is important to realize that in every case, God made the Covenant and called man to obey. Never was a covenant a two-sided "deal".

I should now define and explain the term, "covenant". Typically, a covenant is a solemn agreement between two people or groups, in which each party agrees to act in a certain way, as outlined in the covenant. For example, when a man and woman marry, they make a covenant with each other, by stating vows or promises to each other.

However, when God made the covenants noted below, He acted unilaterally. He prescribed the behavior and duties of the other party, and promised certain things to them. But, the other party (Adam, Abram, Moses, David, etc.) did not sit down with God to arrive at agreement with Him. God acted independent of the other party.

How did God give these covenants, and how did those receiving the covenant get them? Does God make covenants with individuals or people today? God impressed on the minds of the recipients (those to whom the covenant was given) what He wanted them to understand. In the case of Abram, for example, God caused Abram to fall into a deep sleep [**Genesis 15:12**]. On the other hand, Moses was called by God to come to the high part of Mount Sinai, and there God spoke directly with Moses [**Exodus 19:9-24**].

There is no need or point for God to make a covenant with anyone today, for all of His plan is now revealed in the Person of His Son, Jesus, the Christ [**Hebrews 1:1-3**]. His revealing of Himself and His plan is completed in Christ.

Now, let's take a look at the various covenants.

First, there was the covenant with Adam—called the **Adamic Covenant.** This is clearly a covenant, although not expressly called a covenant [**Genesis 1:28-30**]. The key elements of this covenant were:

- Be fruitful and multiply.
- Fill the Earth and subdue it.
- Have (Exercise) dominion over all creatures.

After the Fall [**Genesis 3:1-19**] and the Flood [**Genesis 6:13-8:19**], God made another covenant—with Noah; called the **Noahic Covenant** [**Genesis 9:1-5**]. This covenant was directed again to a single representative of man. It was unilateral. Noah had no part in it except to obey. The Adamic covenant still applied to man, with some modifications. Several elements were added. The key elements of this Covenant were:

- Be fruitful and multiply.
- Fill the Earth.
- Animals will now dread man (and, in some cases, would be hostile to man).
- Animals shall now be food for man. Earlier, man was a vegetarian [**Genesis 1:29-30**].
- Do not eat flesh that is living or containing its blood.
- Institute capital punishment for murder.

Later, God made a Covenant with Abram (Abraham) called the **Abrahamic covenant [Genesis 12:1-3]**. The covenant was addressed to a specific representative of man, and it was unilateral in nature. This covenant was essentially repeated in **[Genesis 17:1-8]**. The key elements were:

- Go to a land God will show you.
- You will become a great, multitudinous nation.
- You will be a blessing to mankind.
- God will bless those who respond favorably to you.
- God will curse those who reject you.
- You will inherit the land God will show you.

This covenant with Abram was later confirmed to his son, Isaac **[Genesis 22:15-18]**, and again later to his grandson, Jacob (Israel) **[Genesis 28:13-14]**.

Some 400 years later, God made a specific **covenant with Moses** (called the **Mosaic Covenant**) **[Exodus 19 to 24]** on behalf of the children of Israel. This was an extended, lengthy covenant which came to be called the "Mosaic Law" or, the "Law of Moses".

This covenant was also directed to an individual representative (Moses) but was applicable only to the children of Israel (the Hebrews), rather than to the whole world. Non-Hebrews (Gentiles) were not under this covenant unless they embraced this Hebrew faith. This covenant was given exclusively for a specific group. The Hebrews were to be witnesses and "priests" to other nations and tribes, on behalf of God.

As a new nation, this covenant provided them with a detailed set of regulations to govern them, politically, socially, economically, ethically and religiously. Again, it was unilateral. The Hebrews were simply to obey. This Covenant served Israel as a Constitution, in effect, for a Theocracy. The major elements of this covenant included:

- A detailed legal system to govern behavior, judgment, and punishment.
- A detailed series of behaviors and attitudes to provide constant symbols and reminders of their special position.
- Dietary limitations and regulations.
- Laws governing the use and ownership of the land.
- Laws governing transgressions and their punishment.
- Laws governing their religious behavior and practices.
- Laws governing their social and economic interactions.

- A sacrificial system designed to show the nature of sin and the remedy for sin.

This covenant was introduced by a sort of preamble; we call this the "Ten Commandments". The **Mosaic covenant** begins with them [**Exodus 20:1-17**], and continues, with some interpolations, throughout the book of Exodus. The books of Leviticus and Numbers provide more details, and Deuteronomy is a basic recapitulation of the Mosaic Law, given to the people as they were about to enter the land originally promised to Abram, Isaac, and Jacob.

We find the next covenant in [**2 Samuel 7:12-16**], some 400 years after the Mosaic Covenant. This, too, was given to an individual, as King and representative of the people of Israel. Here, the promise is narrowed to a single person, a descendant of David. This is called the **Davidic Covenant,** and ultimately will be fulfilled in the Anointed One, Messiah (Christ). The promise was again unilateral, requiring obedience. The key elements were:

- One of David's seed would have an eternal kingdom. That descendant would build a "house" for God's name. He would, if he committed ongoing sins (iniquity), be chastised through the instrumentality of men. In one sense, this would be true of Solomon and the later kings. But it would also apply to Christ, who became the sin-bearer for the world's sin.
- Christ did not commit any sin, but He *literally became full of sin* [**2 Corinthians 5:21**], as man's substitute, when God the Father laid all the sins of all mankind on His Son at the cross of Calvary. But, though this was and is true, God's mercy would never depart from Christ, as demonstrated by His resurrection.

The next (and, last, for the Hebrews) covenant is seen about 450 years later [**Jeremiah 31:31-34**]. This covenant was not directed to an individual, but to a *specific* people: Israel and Judah. At the time this covenant was given, Israel (the 10 tribes) did not even exist as a nation, having been deported by the Assyrians [**2 Kings 17:5-6**]. In fact, after 722 B.C., they never again existed as a nation. Yet the promise is made specifically to them *and* to Judah, who was yet a nation at the time. This covenant is called the **New Covenant.** The key elements were:

- The covenant is a new and future covenant.
- It is specifically directed to Israel and Judah.

- It was to supplant and replace the "old covenant", the Mosaic Covenant.
- God's law will be internalized in the people.
- They will be a faithful people of God.
- Every one of them will personally know God (they will be saved people).
- Their iniquity will be forgiven.
- Their sins will no longer be remembered by God.
- There will be no sacrifices to pay the penalty ("atone") for sin.

This covenant is yet to be fulfilled, as Israel (i.e., the Northern Kingdom—Ephraim) remains a non-existent, (or, at least, unknown) group. The modern nation of Israel stems primarily from the Hebrews of the tribes of Judah and Benjamin, Only God knows where those from the other ten tribes might be.

This covenant is often assumed to be the New Covenant of which Jesus spoke [**1 Corinthians 12:23-26; Matthew 26: 28**]. But, this is not quite accurate, for the Church is neither Israel nor Judah, as we shall see.

So, how are we to understand this? The solution is found in two distinct points.

- In the Covenant outlined in [**Jeremiah 31:31-34**], the covenant is specifically addressed to the nations of Israel and of Judah. God declares them to be His wife, (" . . . though I was a husband to them, says the Lord") [**Jeremiah 31:32**]. Though God declares that their iniquity will be forgiven, no mention is made as to how this will be done, nor does it speak of Messiah. There is no mention of a sacrifice of blood. Of course, other Old Testament passages suggest Messiah's cleansing work, but that is not the focus here in Jeremiah.
- In the Covenant outlined in [**Matthew 26:28-29**], the focus is wholly on the person and work of Messiah, the Lord Jesus Christ. Of course, this is a new covenant in the sense that it is different and the latest presented. However, the thrust is very different from that of Jeremiah thirty-one. The focus in Jeremiah is on what will happen to Israel and Judah in the land. The focus in Matthew is on the sacrificial work of the Messiah for a group of individual believers, who were to be the foundation of a new work, the church.

There are, similarities, in that the believers in this new group, the church, will be indwelt with the Holy Spirit (that is, the Spirit of God will come to indwell the new spirit of the believing one). Thus, the individual's body will itself become a temple of God, as God's Holy Spirit dwells within him. The believer will be "born again", as God provides him with a new nature or new spirit.

These are similar to, but not identical with promises associated with the land of Israel during the Messianic Kingdom. The people of that time will be indwelt, but will also have a temple external to them. However, the similarities do not offset the very different emphases of the two covenantal promises.

The point is: Israel will one day inherit the land, reaping the benefits of the New Covenant of Jeremiah. On the other hand, the church currently experiences some of the features (e.g., indwelling and new birth) that Israel will receive only on the final settling of Israel in the land under the Davidic Messiah-King.

The focus for the New Covenant given to the disciples is the sacrificial atonement of the Lord Jesus. The focus for the New Covenant given to Israel and Judah is on life in the land of Israel under King-Messiah. The latter is described by Matthew as the "Kingdom of Heaven", though this "Kingdom of Heaven" is entirely played out on the Earth.

In other words, these covenants are both new, with similarities, but they are not identical. They have a number of things in common, but are very distinct in their object and focus. It might be inferred that the New Covenant of the New Testament is a derivative of the new covenant in Jeremiah, but we should not assume they are one and the same, for they are not.

Please notice in all the different covenants, there are points held in common:

- All are given unilaterally by God.
- All demand obedience of the recipients.
- Only two are permanent: that of Jeremiah 31 and that of Matthew 26.
- The scope of the recipients varies in the various Covenants. The common thread is God, not the recipients.
- In a number of the Covenants, there are points of similarity. But they are clearly not identical in scope or focus.

Notice further the correlation between the various Covenants and the various Dispensations which God has instituted. (Note: the term "Dispensation" is covered fully in chapter seven. For now, it's sufficient to define a "dispensation" as the "rules of the household" for a particular people for a particular time.)

COVENANT	DISPENSATION
ADAMIC	INNOCENCE
NOAHIC	GOVERNMENT
ABRAHAM	PATRIARCHAL
MOSAIC	LAW
NEW COVENANT(blood)	CHURCH
NEW COVENANT(land)	KINGDOM AGE

The point is that God has developed, from before the foundation of the world, a plan for this earth and for man. This plan is played out over several thousand years and focuses on different peoples at different times. The common thread is that each element is God's unilateral work.

God begins with man, and then narrows the focus down to a specific Semitic tribe, Israel. He further narrows His focus down to a specific Semite, a son of Judah, of the family of David: Messiah. This Messiah is Jesus, the Lord. His focus shifts from men in general to certain groups: first Jew, then a combination of Jew and Gentile into one grouping.

He works at different times in different ways towards different people, but always in accordance with His overall plan. There is no dichotomy, no confusion, and no unplanned deviations. He's in charge from beginning to end, working in history and, indeed, creating history, to accomplish His purposes.

This is especially comforting to realize when considering what is yet to come. God is not a passive observer of the world scene. Neither is He a powerful, but limited, reactor to, or redactor (editor) of, world events. Nor is He an adjusting force or balancing factor in world conditions. No; He is the author and finisher. His plan is working out and will work out exactly as "scripted" in prophecy.

This reminds us that understanding the prophetic books is valuable and helpful to us in various ways, and that much of both Testaments involve prophetic events yet unfulfilled.

- It assures us that God is bringing all to completion and fruition in Christ Jesus.
- It assures us that, no matter the conditions of the day, God is not finished, thwarted, or confused.

- It assures us (as Christians) that how we live and what we do, does matter, as Christ will come again and will meet us at His *Bema* seat [**2 Corinthians 5:9-10; 1 Corinthians 3:13-15**] of judgment, to dispense rewards or pronounce loss of reward.
- It motivates us to urge others to come to Christ now, while there is yet time, for we know His promises of final judgment and divine punishment are not just a figure of speech or an overstatement, but will definitely occur.

With this in mind, we will delve into God's prophetic plan yet to come. We realize that no one can discern all the details and one may not fully comprehend all the details of the events and sequences. Still, so much of the Bible, both Old Testament and New Testament, deals with events yet unfulfilled. We must not ignore them. Indeed, they are necessary to bring us to maturity. They are necessary to equip us for every good work. They are Scripture; they are the Word of God [**2 Timothy 3:16-17**].

We will continue by first examining God's plan and work with Israel in more detail. We will see that God had a specific purpose for this nation that He called. We will observe how they succeeded in certain respects, but failed overall to carry out His plan However, God, in His grace, continues to keep His promises for this people, and will yet carry them out. They have been chastised but have not been cast off forever [**Romans 9 to 11**].

CHAPTER 3

The Chosen People

God might have worked in a broad, general fashion with all the peoples of the world—but He did not do so. Perhaps that's because such an approach could be lost in the maze of humanity. By singling out a particular nation, God could use them as magnificent object lessons, and as demonstrations of the width, depth, and breadth of His Person and Grace. Also, by working in this fashion, this reminds us that He is interested in specific people, not just humanity in the abstract.

God determined to reveal much of His plan and purposes for mankind through His dealings with a small, insignificant tribe of people who were little more than an extended family. He might have chosen mighty Egypt, or powerful Assyria, or some other major player on the world scene. Instead, He chose the extended family of poor Jacob (Israel), a nomadic sheepherder with no pretensions to greatness.

He chose this band of Semites and promised to make of them a great nation, as He had promised Grandfather Abraham and Father Isaac. Still, God did not move quickly on this program. Israel and his family continued to live as transient foreigners in the land of Canaan for quite some time.

Israel's son Joseph had risen to power under the Egyptian Pharaoh, having begun there as a slave. God had Israel and his family move to the land of Goshen, in Egypt, under Joseph's protection. There they lived for some time in peace and plenty.

However, following Joseph's death, the Israelites were gradually turned into servants of the Egyptians and then into abject slaves. This was their lot for some 400 years.

This reminds us that God's timing is not always what we might like, but God's timetable works His purposes, just as He intends. In this case, God was using the crucible of slavery and degradation to bring them to see their need of a deliverer. And it serves as a living, painful illustration of mankind's servitude to sin and their need of a Savior.

Finally, God sent Moses to be their deliverer. He took some 80 years to prepare Moses for this task. Moses was raised in Pharaoh's household, becoming a prince of Egypt. Following his well-intended but foolish attempt to aid his fellow Israelites at age 40, Moses was rejected by the Israelites and pursued by the Egyptians and had to flee for his life. All this is recorded in **[Exodus 2:1-3:1]**.

Moses then spent forty years in Midian, serving as shepherd and son-in-law to Jethro. He apparently made peace with that strange sequel to his privileged life as an Egyptian prince, and carved out a relatively prosperous and peaceful life. But then, God tapped him on the shoulder with the experience of "the burning bush" **[Exodus 3 and 4]**. A most-reluctant Moses was directed to return to Egypt to rescue the Israelites, a task he had attempted on his own initiative forty years earlier.

Notice that God's timetable was some forty years later than that of Moses, and that the Israelites continued to suffer in servitude all that time. It's a reminder that God's plans are often more deliberate than ours. While He keeps His promises, He has a quite different perspective on the issues and solutions then we have. How can a loving God think and act like this, allowing people to continue to suffer, we wonder?

I don't have all the answers to that, but I am reminded of several factors:

1) God is in control of all time, not just *our* lifetime on this earth.
2) Man is not limited to this life alone either. Man will exist forever, and, if saved, will live forever with God.
3) Events and circumstances of this lifetime are but a fragment of man's entire existence. We tend to value and consider everything in relation to this life. God teaches us to consider the life to come.
4) God may permit trials and disasters in this lifetime, but we still belong to Him forever, and He promises justice in the long term.

God used Moses to rescue the Israelites, and began to form them as a nation. In the wilderness of Mount Sinai (also called, "Mount Horeb"), God provided the people with a national constitution, in the form of the "Mosaic

Law" [**Exodus 19 to 24**]. This law was introduced by a preamble of principles, the "Ten Commandments" [**Exodus 20:1-17**]. The law gave specific directions and regulations for all of life, including their political, social, economic, personal, sexual, and familial situations.

The Mosaic Law was designed specifically for the Israelites, for their occupation of the Promised Land, and for a limited time. It was not written for other peoples, but was intended to remind Israelites that they were uniquely chosen by God to be a special people. Their lives were to be a testimony before other peoples, and they were to serve as priests for other peoples, directing the attention of all to God.

God periodically reminded them that they were chosen not because they were so wonderful or so great, but even despite their insignificance. [**Deuteronomy 9:4-6**]. Many of the regulations (such as the dietary laws) were designed to remind the Israelites daily of their special relationship to God.

For example, rabbits were abundant. When a rabbit crossed the path of a Hebrew, he was reminded visually that he was under certain restrictions of God in the Mosaic Law. Likewise, pigs were a favorite meat for Gentiles. Thus, seeing a pig would remind the Jewish person that he was to be different than the Gentiles. Similarly, many of the dietary and other laws were continual reminders to the Hebrew that he was different than the rest of the world.

This great manifesto ruled the people of Israel from their entrance into the land of Canaan (circa 1406 B.C.), until the presentation of Messiah (Christ) to them (circa A.D. 33), some 1400 years.

With the coming of Messiah, the Law was to be fulfilled in Him. The people were no longer under its strictures. Of course, the principles of the Law were still valid expressions of God's holiness and His will, but the regulations were no longer significant in and of themselves.

As Paul put it in Galatians [**Galatians 3:24-25**], the Law was a schoolmaster or discipler of the Israelites until the advent of Messiah. The Law was designed to point out to Israel the necessity of a Savior to finally accomplish for them what the Law could only foreshadow.

No Israelite was ever saved by the keeping of the Law, for none could ever perfectly fulfill it. That is precisely why the sacrificial system and the Day of Atonement were part and parcel of the Law. The writer of the Epistle to the Hebrews emphasizes at length the fact that these sacrifices did not save, but merely anticipated the true salvation through Christ.

In seeking to keep the requirements of the Law, and participating in the sacrificial program, the Israelites were demonstrating their faith in God and His Word, and were depending on *Him* to make them clean. Sadly, for many, the Law became an end in itself, and some presumed that since they were outwardly obeying the Law, they were acceptable to God and were *de facto* saved individuals.

This was the tragic error of the Pharisees. The Pharisees were people of a particular religious sect of Jews in Jesus' day. They went to great lengths to appear to be perfectly keeping the Mosaic Law. Indeed, they thought, and most of the common people agreed, that they (the Pharisees) were the most religious and most ceremonially "clean" people in all of Israel.

In the second chapter of Romans, Paul points out that God is obligated to accept any who perfectly keep the Law (or, who even perfectly keep their own standards). However, in chapter three of Romans, he makes clear that no one has ever done that. Only Christ is perfect; therefore, our perfecting must come through Him.

With the advent of the Lord Jesus Christ, the Jews were to turn to Him, acknowledging Him as the Anointed One Who would save them. Instead, the nation looked to Him as a potential political savior to rescue them from the Romans. When it became clear that this was not Jesus' program, they rejected Him and conspired to have Him slain.

As a result, the nation of Israel (technically, at this point, it was composed of Judah/Benjamin), came under the terrible judgment, beginning with the destruction of Jerusalem in AD 70 and continuing up to the present. That's the bad news; the good news is that God has not cast off His people forever, but will yet save the nation and bring them into Messianic blessings **[Romans 9 through 11]**.

It's now time to examine the history of Israel a little more closely, particularly in regards to the promise of Messiah and the promise of final restoration.

CHAPTER 4

"Messiah is Coming; Hang On!"

A common error we make as Christians, with our ability to view the past, is to assume that what we know about the Christ was also perceived by Israel. We think the Israelites knew basically what we know about Christ (except perhaps for the name "Jesus"), and that they understood the Old Testament prophecies about Christ much as we do.

For example, when we look at [Psalm 22:16b-17a], "... They pierced My hands and My feet; I can count all my bones ...", we realize this is speaking of the crucifixion of the Lord Jesus Christ. But, the Israelites almost certainly did not associate this portion of the Psalm to Christ, or Messiah, and most certainly not to His death.

So, let's look more carefully at what they did know, or could be expected to know, about Messiah. "Christ" is the comparable term to "Messiah". Both mean, "The Anointed One".

Prior to the founding of the people of Israel, in the time of the Fall, God promised a savior to be born of woman [Genesis 3:15]. He was not called Messiah, but that is who is in view. In [Genesis 49:10], there is an allusion to a Savior, who is to come from the tribe of Judah, and who will be called "Shiloh", a term related to the Hebrew term "Shalom" (peace, wholeness). The term "Shiloh" can be translated as "peacemaker".

Later, after the giving of the Mosaic Law and just before the Jews entered the land, they were promised a special prophet. This prophet is described in [Deuteronomy 18:15]. But, this prophet would logically have been viewed as a man, like Moses. And, remember, the time of this is about 1406 B.C., only some 40 years after the Exodus.

Following the occupation of Canaan by the Israelites, there is still no direct mention of a Messiah until sometime after 1004 B.C., when David first ruled all Israel. God promises David that one from his loins would be a mighty, final, eternal and universal king. This is seen in the Davidic Covenant [2 Samuel 7:12-13]. However, most Israelites would see this promise as that of a special king. This glimpse of a Savior/King is given some 400 years AFTER Israel has entered the land.

From the Psalms, most of which date from the time of David, it is obvious that there is some understanding of a great person, one who would be unique, and could even be divine. This is obvious from passages such as [Psalm 2:7; 8:4-5; 16:10; Psalms 22, 23, 24; 45:6-7; 68:18; and 110:1-4].

However, the Israelites seem generally to have understood this person to be a political and social savior/king, who would bring Israel unprecedented greatness on this earth. He was not perceived as a Savior from sin.

Viewing the prophetic books in their chronological order, we find Micah speaking of the location of the birth of the coming Savior [Micah 5:2]. This ruler was to be born in Bethlehem, the city of David. Micah's prophecy can be dated about 735-710 B.C., some 300 years after the Davidic Covenant and the Psalms.

It is the prophet Isaiah who first sketches most vividly and thoroughly the outlines of this Savior. It is difficult to read some of these passages [e.g., Isaiah 9, 11, 53] and not see the divinity and indeed the authority of Messiah. Yet the Jewish people tended to continue to view the coming Messiah as a David "writ large".

Some of the key Messianic passages in Isaiah include: [Isaiah 7:14; 9:6-7; chapter 11; 16:5; 19:20; 22:22; 42:1-3,5-8; chapter 53; 59:16-18, 20; and 61:1-2]. While there are many other passages that, from our better-informed perspective, clearly apply to Messiah, these passages are perhaps the most clear and unequivocal revelations about Messiah given to the Jews to that point.

Next, we have Zephaniah speaking of Messiah [Zephaniah 3:17]. Then Jeremiah adds significant fleshing out of the portrait of Messiah [Jeremiah 23:5-6 and 33:15]. Zephaniah writes in 630 B.C., and Jeremiah's writings follow shortly thereafter.

Of course, we have a tremendously-important addition to the picture of Messiah and His reign [Daniel 9:25-27]. It's important to see that Messiah is identified as Messiah. He is perceived as a unique prince who will come to Israel in some later time, after terrible tragedies occur to the nation.

About 480-470 B.C., the prophet Zechariah gives more startling details about Messiah and His coming. It is preceded by terrible judgments on the people and land. Messiah is seen as supernatural in His Person and Power. We see this in [**Zechariah 6:12-13 and 9:9**], followed by harrowing, detailed descriptions [**Zechariah 12:10; 14:4,9,16**]. The coming of Messiah to Israel is to be ushered in by a cataclysmic judgment.

Cementing this thought, Malachi warns that the coming of Messiah will be associated with that terrible day of judgment, the **"Day of the Lord"**, and will be preceded by an Elijah-like messenger [**Malachi 3:1-2; 4:2-6**]. The good news is that this Messiah is seen as the "Sun of righteousness" [**Malachi 4:2**] who shall have "healing in his wings". This provides assurance that Israel shall prosper and blossom magnificently.

The Old Testament provides many insights into the Person and Work of the Christ, but these may generally be read as describing one who is merely the greatest Israelite, one who would provide Israel with unprecedented greatness and power. Passages like those in [**Isaiah 9 and 11**], which could only be describing Deity, were reduced to the longed-for hope of political and social independence and power.

The idea of needing a Savior from sin was alien to their thinking, as they considered themselves to be God's special people, and therefore okay. This is why they were so offended when Jesus insisted they personally required cleansing. Isaiah fifty-three speaks of the servant, obviously identified as Messiah, suffering for the sins of the people of Israel.

Yet, amazingly, Israelites of that day, and, indeed, Israelites of today see that servant as none other than the nation itself. How the nation suffers to "save" the nation is a bit of a mystery, but they make that connection nonetheless. For the alternative must be to accept Messiah as Savior for one's sins.

The focus of Israel was always on the land and on the primacy of their nation. And, indeed, as promised, the nation will one day receive such an exalted condition. But, to an Israelite, the idea of a personal, individual salvation simply was not in view. True, Moses and others realized that, as [**Hebrews 11:39**] reminds us, but this was not the thought pattern of those in Israel.

Thus, for those Israelites heeding the call of John the Baptist to repentance and baptism, this was a very bold and brave step indeed. Likewise, when Peter, in Acts two, called the Israelites to personal repentance and the need to change their identity and allegiance (as the nation was now under God's judgment), this was an immense step to take.

Since the idea of a national resurgence and exaltation was such a major element in Jewish thinking, we shall turn to a consideration of this, seeking out the relevant passages and examining just what they promised and taught.

One final note: we should not be too harsh in our assessment of the Jews' failure to grasp the implications of Messiah. We Christians also tend to be highly-selective in our consideration of the Word at times.

For example, the Scriptures are quite clear on such matters as adultery, divorce, homosexuality, among other issues. Yet some Christians tend to adjust the teachings to accommodate what is more palatable. Some squirm under the teaching that there is only one way to God, through Jesus Christ. We see devout neighbors and 'good' people around us worshipping Allah, Krishna, or perhaps even Mother Nature. We flinch from insisting that there is only one way of salvation—through accepting the finished work of the Lord Jesus Christ.

CHAPTER 5

Things to Come

In tracing the outline of what is going to happen, we need to keep track of two important points:

1. We need to trace matters in a logical, chronological fashion, so we can see the prophetic picture unfolding in a coherent fashion.
2. We need to understand that the prophets, under the inspiration of the Holy Spirit, tended to mix the short term picture with a longer view, particularly in regards to the matter of judgment of Israel. For example, the tribulation experience of Judah in the 70 years captivity is intermingled often with events that clearly did not occur during or near that episode, but refer to the **"Day of the Lord"** yet to come.

We should also understand that, in dealing with prophecy, interpreting details and placing precise timing is a chancy venture, at best. I appreciate that one might err in some details, but I believe strongly that the broad, overall picture sketched here is basically accurate.

Here is the essential grid of what is to come, AFTER the 70 years captivity, and after Israel returns to the land following that captivity. Of course, when we use the term "Israel", we are really referring to the people of Judah and Benjamin, for they are the people who went into captivity in Babylon. The other 10 tribes had earlier been transported to Assyria in 722 B.C.. Following this listing, we will flesh it out and provide Scripture references for you to check out for yourself.

- Elijah (or, someone in the spirit and power of Elijah) will come as a forerunner of Messiah.
- Messiah will be a personage born of the house of David, in the town of Bethlehem, and will be the ultimate king on that throne.
- He will present Himself to His people, but will be rejected and scorned.
- He will be cut off and executed.
- However, Messiah will also be a conquering king accepted by the people. (This is a paradox that we will need to examine further.)
- This victorious Messiah will come following a time of great tribulation for the people of Israel, and will prove victorious over the Gentiles in a great battle.
- This time of great tribulation is called "the **Day of the Lord**". It is an extended period of terror and judgment on Israel.
- When the **Day of the Lord** is completed and Messiah is enthroned, there will be a resurrection of Old Testament saints. They will inhabit the newly-established kingdom on this earth, along with living, redeemed Jews and Gentiles. This will constitute a Messianic reign of unimaginable greatness.

This Messianic Kingdom has a number of important features:

- It will be located on this earth.
- It will consist of saved Israelites and saved Gentiles who are still alive at the end of the judgments.
- It will also include resurrected Old Testament saints.
- David shall be resurrected and will be the Prince of the Jewish people, under Messiah.
- The temple will be rebuilt and temple services shall be restored. These will be similar to those of the Mosaic Law, but with some significant differences. For example, there will be no Yom Kippur (Day of Atonement).
- Every person who is brought into the Messianic Kingdom will be filled with the outpoured Holy Spirit.
- Life will be long-lasting. In fact, it may be that few people will die during this time, apart from those summarily executed as rebels by direction of the Messiah.
- There shall be strict and swift justice, with Messiah being Judge, Jury, and Executioner.

- Jerusalem will be the center of government by Messiah.
- Gentiles will come up to Jerusalem to worship with the Jews. They will worship Messiah.

In presenting this, I've left out New Testament information which could flesh this out even more. We will deal with that later. At this point, I want to reconstruct what any devout Jew in the time of John the Baptist *should* know. In fact, however, they made many errors of judgment regarding these prophetic Scriptures.

Now, let's begin to examine each point, considering them in more detail.

Elijah (or, someone in the spirit and power of Elijah) will come as a forerunner of Messiah. Scriptures:[Isaiah 40:3-5; Malachi 3:1; Malachi 4:5-6].

He will introduce Messiah BEFORE the beginning of the **Day of the Lord**. This messenger will seek to turn Israel to accept Messiah.

This poses serious problems for one studying Messiah in the Old Testament alone. Zechariah, for example, shows Messiah coming at the END of the judgments of the **Day of the Lord.** Such confusion, along with other passages such as Isaiah fifty-three, caused some Jewish scholars to posit two Messiahs. One would suffer and one would conquer.

Messiah will be a personage born of the house of David, in the town of Bethlehem, and will be the ultimate king on that throne. Scriptures: [2 Samuel 7:12-16; Micah 5:2; Isaiah 9:5-6; Psalm. 2:7].

The Davidic Covenant [2 Samuel 7:12-16] could not refer ultimately to Solomon for it is a kingdom to be established FOREVER, and Solomon's kingship died out with Coniah, as we shall see.

There are many related passages that see Messiah as the ultimate King. He is called God, in effect [Isaiah 9:5-6], but a God who is **born**! Elsewhere, He is called the Branch [e.g., Isaiah 11:1-10] who is clearly divine with omnipotent, ultimate authority.

He will present Himself to His people, but will be rejected and scorned. Scriptures: [Isaiah 51; Isaiah 52; Isaiah 53].

Passages such as Isaiah fifty-three were difficult and confusing for the Jews, as this suggested both that Messiah would "fail" and die, and that the people of Israel required His sacrificial death in order to be in right standing with Jehovah. Since they perceived themselves as God's chosen, they could not reconcile this need with their presumed status. As a result, they sometimes developed the idea of a suffering Messiah, to be followed by a conquering

Messiah. Later, Jewish scholars saw Israel itself as the "Servant" in these passages, "saving" themselves by their trials and tribulations.

This person will be cut off and executed. Scriptures: [Isaiah 53; Psalm 22].

This was (and, is) one of the most puzzling, confusing aspects of the role of Messiah to the Jews. Messiah must be human, if He is to die. Yet He is often equated with God, given the title "Lord". Elaborate explanations have been developed to explain this away. Jews today tend to see the Isaiah passage as referring to the nation itself suffering and dying (. . . for the nation?).

It is quite clear, however, that Messiah will give His life sacrificially for the sins of His people. Accordingly, many Jews concluded that there must be two Messiahs, one who would die, and one who would rule victoriously.

However, Messiah will also be a conquering king accepted by the people. This is a paradox: how can Messiah be both a conquering king and a rejected sacrifice? Scriptures: [Isaiah 9:6-7; Isaiah 11:1-16; Zechariah 14:3-9].

Promises such as these were much more palatable to the people of Israel. Here is the successful, glorious king who would rescue, restore, and enrich the nation. Still, even here, there is a bit of confusing terminology, as it is difficult to distinguish between a human Messiah and the Lord God Himself.

The Jews tended to think of Messiah as a larger-than-life King David. For a monotheist to think of Messiah in precisely the same terms as Jehovah God was difficult, even ridiculous, although throughout their Scriptures this paradox was often presented.

Nonetheless, Messiah could be seen as one ushering in a glorious age. Until the prophecies of Daniel, however, the Israelite could imagine a resurrection of those Jews living prior to this glorious kingdom only dimly, if at all. Daniel makes clear that all believing Jews will be resurrected at the time of the establishment of the Kingdom **[Daniel 12:1-2]**. (Unbelieving Jews will be resurrected at the Great White Throne Judgment.) Prior to this, very little was said or implied about a resurrection. Job (not an Israelite) seemed to suggest that he expected to be resurrected **[Job 13:15,16 and Job 15:13-14]**. David also seemed to believe this **[2 Samuel 12:20-23]**.

This victorious Messiah will come following a time of great tribulation for the people of Israel, and will prove victorious over the Gentiles in a great battle. Scriptures: [Daniel 9:24-27; Daniel 11:36-12:1; Zechariah 12 through 14].

The message of the **"Day of the Lord"** is one of the most awesome prophecies in all of Scripture (in the New Testament as well as in the Old

Testament). This describes an unprecedented time of devastation and judgment to come upon the whole world, especially upon Israel. Some people assume this refers to the Babylonian captivity, but this cannot be, for several reasons:

The prophetic scope and details do not fit the details and events of the Babylonian captivity. They are much more severe and are more universal, not limited, in their scope. Many of the prophecies were given AFTER the time of the Babylonian captivity (605-530 B.C.). Jeremiah (and, probably, Habakkuk) prophesied about and during the time of the Captivity. Ezekiel and Daniel were written in the midst of that captivity, and describe future events. Haggai, Zechariah, and Malachi were penned subsequent to that time.

From the perspective of Christians, the "**Day of the Lord**" is mentioned often in the Gospels and in many of the Epistles, and is obviously future. And, clearly, this is the same "**Day of the Lord**" described in the Old Testament. This time of Great Tribulation is called "The **Day of the Lord**". It is an extended period of terror and Judgment on Israel.

There is no more extensive or detailed subject in all of Scripture than that of "The **Day of the Lord**" (See the Appendix). This is an extended period of time beginning with the advent of unprecedented troubles for the people of Israel and continuing up to the advent of the victorious Messiah. The Gentiles are also judged during this period.

This theme is also carried on extensively in the New Testament, although the church is specifically excluded [**1 Thessalonians 5:1-11**]. The church is seen only in heaven, not on the earth during the terrible seal, trumpet, and vial judgments of Revelation. When Jesus speaks of this period [**Matthew 24**], He addresses specifically the nation of Israel, and the disciples as representatives of that nation, for the church had not yet been formed.

When the **Day of the Lord** is completed and Messiah is enthroned, there will be a resurrection of Old Testament saints, who will then inhabit the newly-established kingdom on this earth. This will institute a Messianic reign of unimaginable greatness. Scriptures: [**Daniel 12:1-2; Job 13:15-16; Job 15:13-15**].

Somewhat surprisingly, there is very little indication or information about a bodily resurrection in the Old Testament. There are perhaps several reasons:

- The focus provided by God for the Jews is life on this planet in human (mortal) form. The promises are earthly: long life, material plenty, a future for descendants, etc. Their inheritance was seen as earthly and material. This does not mean that there would be no other future for Israel, but simply that the focus for them was to be on the "here and now".

- Without a full revelation of the Person and Work of Christ (Messiah), a message of bodily resurrection would hardly be clear and meaningful. A focus on resurrection alone might suggest a future not unlike that of later Islam, where one would have a larger-than-life, but still very human event. The focus would then be on the physical always, rather than the spiritual.

  o This error is avoided among the New Testament saints due to the indwelling presence of the Holy Spirit and focus on things above. But the promise of the Holy Spirit for the Israelites was to **follow** the Great Tribulation.

- The Messianic (Millennial) Kingdom is to be populated by human beings in their mortal bodies. If a heavy emphasis were put on resurrection in the Old Testament prophecies, Israelites would not likely have much interest in prophecies which speak of a long, fruitful life in the Messianic Kingdom. Rather, they would be more interested in being resurrected, whatever that might involve.

  o However, as Daniel makes plain, there will indeed be resurrected saints in this Messianic Kingdom. These will be those who have died before the Messianic Kingdom has been instituted.

Other salient facts about the Messianic Kingdom can be seen:

- This Messianic Kingdom will be focused on this earth. If anything is clear in the Old Testament, it is the fact that the Messianic Kingdom will be on the earth—not on some newly-formed earth, but on the existing earth.

  o This conclusion is inevitable if one takes the words of the Old Testament prophecies at face value. The only way to escape this is to "spiritualize" or allegorize most of the Old Testament prophecies. This is done by Amillennial Christians and Covenant Premillennial Christians in order to accommodate these passages to their particular view of the Church. The amazing thing is that they are usually very insistent on a natural, normal interpretation of all other Scripture passages.

- Another feature of the Messianic Kingdom is that it will consist of saved Israelites and saved Gentiles who are still alive at the end of the judgments.
- This Kingdom is an earthly kingdom, populated by people who have never died. They will have children, plant fields, build buildings, and carry on commerce. This would hardly be true of resurrected saints in heaven.
- There is no indication of the duration of this Kingdom in the Old Testament, other than that it seems to be "forever". On the other hand, in the New Testament we find that its duration will be one thousand years. We also learn that ultimately there will be a new heaven and a new earth.

  o   It is nonetheless logical and accurate that the Old Testament should speak of Messiah's Kingdom as everlasting or eternal, for that is truly the case. When the Millennial (1000 year) reign [**Revelation 20:1-7**] is complete, the Kingdom *of God* shall continue on eternally in the new heavens and new earth, as Revelation chapters 21 and 22 indicate. In other words, Messiah's kingdom shall be eternal, divided into one thousand years of primarily earthly rule, followed by eternity.

- It shall also include resurrected Old Testament saints [**Daniel 12:1-2**]. From this passage, it is clear that departed Old Testament saints (those whom the Lord has saved) will also participate in the Messianic Kingdom. We are not given much information about just how this will work out. The presumption is that they will assist David and the Lord Jesus in the administration of the kingdom, serving as an example of God's grace and power
- David himself will be resurrected and shall serve as the Prince of Israel, under the King of Kings and Lord of Lords, Messiah Himself [**Hosea 3:5; Ezekiel 34:23 and 37:25; Jeremiah 30:9**].

  o   Although the Messiah is truly a Messiah for the Jews, His dominion and authority ranges much further—over all of redeemed humanity.

Thus, David the King will be restored as King over Israel and Prince under the Messiah.

o   Often, Christians assume that these references refer to Jesus Christ, although David is specifically mentioned. This is another example of not taking the plain language of the Bible at face value. Since these passages declare that David will be the King and since Daniel asserts that the Old Testament saints will be raised, what else would David be expected to be? And, why would Messiah, clearly portrayed as a world-wide ruler, be seen to be limited to Kingship over Israel?

• The Temple shall be rebuilt and some temple practices restored **[Ezekiel 40-48]**. These passages are sometimes ridiculed as some say that restoration of sacrifices would be unnecessary and indeed abominable with the advent of the rule of Messiah. But, nothing would be more natural for Israel than to resume these practices, if one takes note of the changes and adjustments made **[Ezekiel 40-48]**.

• There will be no Day of Atonement. There will be no Scapegoat ceremony; no sacrificial lamb slain. Sacrifices will be offered for unintentional sin. (The sacrifices for sin outlined in the Mosaic Law were always and only for *unintentional* sins.Only on the Day of Atonement was there provision for wilful sins.) This is logical, for the living Israelites are still human beings who may unintentionally err. If they provide a sin offering, they shall continue in fellowship. If they sin wilfully in opposing Messiah, He will immediately judge them and cut them off.

• There are not two holy places—the Holy Place and the Holy of Holies, as before, but only the Most Holy Place.

We will have more on the Messianic Kingdom later, after we've reviewed New Testament teaching.

CHAPTER 6

"Setting the Plate"

Daniel nine, especially the last few verses, is very important. This is such an important part of the overall end times "quilt" that we must give it more careful attention at this point. If you don't understand [Daniel 9:24-27] and its significance, you won't understand the end times at all. Or, at least, you will not gain a true biblical perspective.

As we should always do when studying a passage of Scripture, we must consider the context first. First, we will study the man; and, then, the times in which he writes.

I begin with the conviction that Daniel really wrote Daniel (after all, the Lord Jesus thought so [Matthew 24:15]). He wrote in the period from 605 B.C. to perhaps 525 B.C.

Daniel was taken as a captive/hostage from Judea by the Babylonians when they first invaded Judea in 605 B.C. As a very young teen, Daniel was taken to provide service to the Babylonian court. He was undoubtedly made a eunuch, a custom of the day for slaves working in the service of the court. He lived a very long life, seeing the effects of the second and third deportations of Judeans to Babylon (597 B.C. and 586 B.C.). He probably knew Ezekiel, who was taken in the second deportation.

Daniel realizes that the prophesied seventy years of captivity is about to end [Jeremiah 25:11-12; 29:10]. Daniel is now an old man, still longing for the freedom for his people to return to the Promised Land. Some sixty-six years have now elapsed, starting with 605 B.C. This chapter is dated as the first year of Darius the son of Ahasuerus, which would make the date about 539 B.C.

Daniel, long a man of prayer, now sets himself to beseech God to fulfill His promise. He is candid about the unworthiness and sins of his people. He asks God to act, not in pity for their sakes, but for God's own sake and His character [Daniel 9:16-19]. His prayers are answered, but in a quite unexpected manner, by the angel Gabriel. I say "unexpected" because the answer makes clear that there will be a long period of strife and stress before Israel is finally rescued. This and subsequent revelations caused Daniel much distress [e.g., Daniel 10:3, 8-9, 16-17].

Here, then, is the prophecy recorded in [Daniel 9:24-27] which provides such an amazing timetable of things to come.

It begins with, "Seventy weeks . . .". The term translated as "weeks" literally means "seven". So, 70x7 = 490. But, 490 what? Weeks? Months? Years? Decades?. Well, it's simple to rule out weeks and months, for nothing in history subsequent to the beginning date could fit. In a moment, we shall learn that the beginning date is well-established, although it is unknown to Daniel. However, as we shall see, considering this 490 as "years" not only fits well, but is astoundingly accurate!

At the climax of the 490 "years", several things will be true for Jerusalem, Judea and Israel:

- The transgression of the Hebrews will be ended.
- There will be an end of sins (for the Hebrews, at least).
- Their iniquity will be reconciled (with God).
- They will experience an everlasting righteousness.
- Visions and prophecies will be fulfilled.
- The Most Holy (One) will be anointed [Messiah].

Now, we have a bit of a problem. None of these things has yet happened! But, let's move on.

In verse 25, we find the beginning, the *terminus a quo*. It is dated from "the going forth of the command to restore and build Jerusalem . . ." When did this happen? Not in the lifetime of Daniel, although some Jews were permitted to return after 630 B.C.

The command to restore and build was given, not by the Babylonians, but by their later conqueror, the Persians. Nehemiah, a Jew, records this [Nehemiah 2:1-9]. This is reliably dated as either 445 or 444 B.C., in the days of Nehemiah and Ezra.

Thus, our starting point for this 490 years would be 445 B.C. (or, 444, perhaps). There appears to be an ending point noted in the middle part of verse

25, at least until we read further. Since many events are described subsequent to "Messiah the Prince", this cannot truly be the *terminus ad quem*, or the end point of the 490 years. Good thing, too, for Messiah came in ministry about A.D. 30-33, which allows for only some 478 years (445 B.C. to A.D. 33, when Jesus was executed). So we must procede cautiously.

The last part of verse 25, provides a new timing mystery. He speaks of seven "sevens" and sixty-two "sevens". Assuming our preliminary idea that a "seven" refers to seven years, we have to somehow account for a forty-nine year period and a period of 434 years (62x7). Should we add these to the 475 year period, or could they be components within the 478 year period? We must consider the rest of the prophecy to determine this.

The prophecy indicates that "after the sixty-two weeks, Messiah shall be cut off, but not for Himself." Assuming Jesus is the Messiah, His sacrificial death occurred in A.D. 33, according to most accounts. So the sixty-two weeks must be worked in prior to that event.

Thus, it must be part of the 490 year period. Indeed, it must be part of the 478 year period we have tentatively developed. Logically, then, the "seven sevens" must also fit within that time frame. Let's continue on with our major problem, and later we'll return to a possible explanation of the seven and the sixty-two.

Verse 26 says that the city and the temple (sanctuary) will be destroyed, after Messiah has been cut off. This destruction occurred in A.D. 70, when the Romans levelled the city and temple, as Jesus had said would happen [Matthew 23:37-24:2]. If we add 70 to 445, we get a sum of 515; that doesn't fit the known facts.

However, if we go back to the 478 year plan, we are still 12 years short of the prescribed 490 years. What shall we do? Well, the prophecy is not yet completely considered, so let's plow forward, and come back to this dilemma when all the data are in.

The last verse speaks of "he shall confirm a covenant with many for one seven". This must be the last seven years of the 490 years. Therefore, we need to find 483 years from the decree in Nehemiah two to the crucifixion of Christ, not the 490 we earlier anticipated.

But, Who is this "he"? The immediate antecedant would be the prince spoken of earlier in the verse. This prince is connected with the people who destroyed the city—the Romans. Thus, He must have some connection with the Roman Empire? But this prince did not destroy the city; his people did. And no Roman authority made any covenant with the Jews following the destruction of the city.

Therefore, this prince must have some kind of Roman origin, and he would come sometime later than the destruction of A.D. 70. The answer to this conundrum will be found in the prophecies of the kingdoms, recorded in Daniel seven. We'll look at that a bit later.

Back to our dating dilemma: It is well known that the Jewish calendar consisted of twelve 30-day months; a lunar calendar. Periodically, they added a month to balance it with the solar calendar. So, if we take 483 years times 360 days (one year), we arrive at 173,880 days.

Sir Robert Anderson wrote a very interesting book on this subject, entitled "The Coming Prince" around the beginning of the 20th Century. He determined that the decree of Nehemiah occurred in March 14, 445, and he calculated the entry of Jesus into Jerusalem [Matthew 21:1-11] as occurring on April 6, A.D. 32. Adding in for 116 leap year days and a 24 day period from March 14 to April 6, he arrived at 173,880 days! An uncanny coincidence?

But, remember, I suggested that Jesus actually entered in A.D. 33? I did this deliberately to make a point. Remember also, that I said the Nehemiah date could be 444 B.C.? My point is that would be approximately the same number of days. Thus, using our calendar, and using 483 years, we get a remarkable correlation. I do not know if each date is precisely accurate, but the coincidence of numbers of days is quite telling. Personally, I think this cements the idea of the "seven" equalling seven years, and makes this a remarkably precise prophecy

With this, we have the issue of dating resolved. But, wait, what about the "seven" and the "sixty-two"? I don't have an assured answer, but something I read (I cannot recall where) suggested this may refer to the opening of Herod's Temple. Although this temple was not completed until just before the Romans tore it down in A.D. 70, it had been in regular use since about 16 B.C. Herod had taken the temple rebuilt on the site of Solomon's Temple, and had greatly expanded and beautified it. In or about 16 B.C., he opened it for regular use.

So what? Well, from 445 B.C. until 16 B.C. is 429 years; very close to our 434 years found in the "sixty-two" sevens, perhaps not precise, but remarkably close. And, from 16 B.C. until A.D. 33 is 49 years, which matches the "seven sevens".

Is Daniel's prophecy in this regard alluding to the opening of the Temple? I don't know, but it seems to fit better than any other scenario I can imagine.

Before we move away from this, we need to briefly consider the kingdoms prophesied in Daniel seven, to round out our understanding.

Daniel seven is dated about 550 B.C [**Daniel 7:1**], just before Babylon was conquered by the Persians. Daniel had this strange dream along with an interpretation. Basically, the dream involved six kingdoms, although we usually think of just four.

The first kingdom was that of Babylon, represented by the first beast, a lion-like creature with eagles' wings. The lion and eagle were symbols widely used by Babylon.

The second was pictured by a bear, which was humped or raised up on one side, and had three ribs in its mouth. This represented the twin kingdom of Medo-Persia. The Persians were dominant over the Medes, as depicted by the "lop-sided" aspect. The three ribs would have been the kingdoms of Babylon, Lydia, and Egypt, each conquered by Medo-Persia.

The third beast was seen as a Leopard with four wings. This represented the kingdom of Alexander the Great. His kingdom was divided among his four key generals, following Alexander's premature death. Chapter eight of Daniel confirms, with somewhat different beastly representations, that Medo-Persia and Greece are in view [**Daniel 8:18-22**]. This also gives us information about the fourth beast, Rome. At the time Daniel saw this, Rome was not a power at of any significance.

The fourth beast was most unusual and more powerful than the others had been. The significant feature was its ten horns, from among which came a "little horn", who we have identified with the Great Man.

The reason I say there are six kingdoms is that the fifth is that constituted by the "little horn" and the sixth is the eternal Kingdom of the Son of Man. This "little horn" is, I believe, the same prince described in [**Daniel 9:26**].

The title, "Son of Man", is defined in [**Daniel 7:13-14**] and represents the eternal kingdom of Messiah. This passage explains why Jesus often referred to himself as the "Son of Man", as recorded in the Gospel accounts.

[**Daniel 7:7-8**] is a primary basis for the idea of a powerhouse arising out of the ashes of the Roman Empire, and headed by one who seized power from three other powers, in a ten nation "confederacy". This might be a revived Roman Empire, or, more likely, a nation and nations generating from the original portions of that Empire. Thus, it is conceivable, for instance, that the United States could be part of that remnant, as our history goes back to England who was once part of the Roman Empire.

This information, coupled with other points noted elsewhere in our study, helps to flesh out some of the background for the events of the end times.

CHAPTER 7

"What is this Dispensation stuff?"

W e have seen that God has been and is working differently in different periods. We saw this in the covenants and in the narrowing relationships as God first works with a broad spectrum of man, narrows to Abraham, then to Israel, and finally to Christ, His Messiah. Now let's examine this in more detail, and see clearly just what God is doing and how He's doing it.

First, we must understand that there is a sense in which God has only one plan—to wrap up everything in Christ. We see this in passages such as [Psalm 2:6-12; Isaiah 9:6-7; Isaiah 11; Daniel 7:13-14; Philippians 2:9-11; and, Hebrews 1:1-3]. There has always been, and always will be, only one way to acceptance with God the Father. That is through the work of His Son, Jesus, the Christ. This is most important to understand: there is, and always has been, only ONE way of salvation—through the Lord Jesus Christ.

No Old Testament Jew was ever saved by or through the Law. Abraham was not saved apart from the sacrificial work of Christ. All Old Testament saints, Jew or Gentile, were saved on the basis of the finished work of Christ on the cross at Calvary, although that event was unknown to them during their lifetimes. It was always God's plan that Christ's death on the cross would be the only way to justify the ungodly while also justifying God's wrath and judgment on man.

We will see that God has acted in differing ways with different generations and groups, but *always* on the basis of Christ's finished work. We will call these different ways, **Dispensations**, the term the Bible uses for a number of them. These are just different ways God has of dealing with people at a certain period of time.

First, all Christians would agree that there are two Dispensations—the Old, and the New. These would correlate to the Old Testament or Old Covenant, and the New Testament or New Covenant. The question is, are there any others?

The term "dispensation" in the Greek is **oikonomia** [oikonomia]. It means, "stewardship", "management of a household" (literally, "law of the household"). This term is used in [**Luke 16:2-4**], where it is translated "stewardship". It is also used in [**1 Corinthians 9:17; Ephesians 1:10; 3:2**], where it is translated as "dispensation". It is translated as "dispensation" in [**Colossians 1:25**].

Now, the question is, how many different "dispensations" or "stewardships" are there in God's plan? This does NOT mean different ways of salvation, but different ways of God's dealing (primarily with God's saved people) at different times.

Certainly, God was saving people before the time of the Mosaic Law (which is typically thought of as the "Old Covenant". The Mosaic Law, as we have seen, was directed specifically to a certain people, the Hebrews. How did God deal with people prior to the Mosaic Law? Clearly, He did so in a different manner. Thus, we have a "PRE-LAW" dispensation.

So, now we have the following dispensations:

- Pre-Law
- Law
- New Covenant (Church)

But, wait! Did God always deal the same with man in the "Pre-Law" 'era? Remember our study of the covenants. He dealt differently with man after the Flood than He did before the Flood. So, we need to divide the "Pre-Law" dispensation:

- Pre-Flood
- Post-Flood
- Law
- Church

Now we have four dispensations. But, does this satisfy all the facts of the Old Testament? Not quite. For God dealt differently with Adam before the Fall and Adam and his offspring following the Fall. Therefore, we may refine our groupings a bit more, like this:

- Pre-Fall ("innocence")
- Post-Fall (but Pre-Flood)
- Post-Flood
- Law
- Church

Still, as we think this through, it hardly seems accurate to say that God dealt the same with all men after the flood, but before the Law. Following Noah, who represented all of eight people (all mankind, after the flood), God began to narrow His workings to a specific group, beginning with Abraham. So, let's factor that in:

- Pre-Fall [innocence]
- Post-Fall [conscience; knowledge of evil (Man had already known Good—God]
- Post-Flood [human government]
- Patriarchal Period [Abraham *et al*]
- Law
- Church

Now, we have **six** dispensations, each identifiable in differing ways. But, we're not quite done yet. The era I labelled as "Church" has differing components also. If it is true that the Church will be completed with the Rapture, just before the Tribulation period, then we must say that God is going to work a bit differently following that event. (Even if we were to ignore the Rapture issue, the Kingdom Age differs significantly from the Church Age, since in that Kingdom Age, Messiah will be ruling on Earth.) So, now we have:

- Pre-Fall [innocence]
- Post-Fall [conscience]
- Post-Flood [human government]
- Patriarchal Period [Abraham et al]
- Law
- Church age
- Messianic Kingdom era

We now have seven clearly identifiable eras where the management of man differed significantly.

Notice how these seem to correlate with our previous analysis of the various Covenants (chapter 2). Perhaps this little chart will help:

Covenants	Dispensations
Adamic	Innocence
	Conscience (post-Fall)
Noahic	Human Government
Abrahamic	Patriarchs
Mosaic	Law
Davidic	(promise of Kingdom)
New Covenant (blood)	Church
New Covenant (land)	Messianic Kingdom

With this broad outline in view, we need to consider the details of the governing relationships for each dispensation. But, before we do, we should clear up some confusion generated among Christians who do not accept the idea of more than two dispensations. Usually, these people get the idea of only two dispensations from what is termed "Reformed Theology".

Reformed theologians may be broadly represented by Luther and Calvin, among others. As they sought to "reform" the Roman Catholic Church, they retained much of the basic theology of that institution. After all, they were reformers, not revolutionaries. In modern history, the Reformed Theology is represented by institutions like Presbyterianism and the Christian Reformed Church.

Some groups with an Arminian background, such as Methodists, Pentecostals, Charismatics, and others, also often accept the doctrine of only two dispensations. Some Pentecostals and Charismatics have simultaneously embraced the doctrines of the Rapture and the Millennial Kingdom, blending these with the two covenant theory. This is quite inconsistent, but not unusual in their practices.

In any event, the basic Reformed Theology perspective is this: There are two Covenants (they don't care much for the term "dispensation"): the Covenant of Works and the Covenant of Grace. They see the Covenant of Works as that preceding the Fall, and everything else falls under the Covenant of Grace. Of course, you will search the Scriptures in vain for those two Covenants. They simply are not there. They must be inferred.

Nonetheless, it's a bit difficult to see how all the variations of God's dealings with man since the Fall can fit neatly into one Covenant. It's also a bit confusing when you realize that these same people make sharp distinctions between Israel and the Church. They see the Mosaic Law period as that controlled by "Law" and the current age as that controlled by "Grace".

Though I honor and respect the great Christian teachers and theologians through the ages who have held such views, I must courteously and firmly disagree with them. Their attempt to retain the basic teachings and practices of the Roman Church since Augustine, especially in the areas of Ecclesiology (the nature of the church) and Eschatology (the study of the End Times), has caused them to shove all the eras into one theological strait-jacket.

They like to believe that the Church is the New Testament version of Israel, and that the End Times are likely to be condensed into one event—the return of Christ. Typically, they believe that Christ will usher in the new heavens and new earth, without a millennial kingdom or a period of great tribulation. We recognize that this is a prevalent view among many Christian groups, so we have an obligation to be very clear when we differ from it.

With that, let us begin a more detailed consideration of the various dispensations.

The Dispensation of Innocence

This is the "pre-Fall" era with Adam and Eve. In this, God gives several instructions to them:

- Be fruitful and multiply.
- Leave and Cleave (marriage).
- Fill the Earth and Subdue it.
- Exercise dominion over all creatures.

The Dispensation of Conscience

This is "post-Fall", but "pre-Flood".

- Man now had 'independent' knowledge of Good and Evil (or, conscience).
- He was removed from the Garden of Eden and from God's direct presence.

- God used the life of animals to make clothing for man (prefiguring sacrifice.)
- He was to make offerings to God.
- Relationships between man and woman, and between man and the earth were made more difficult.
- The following earlier commands still applied:

  o Be fruitful and multiply.
  o Leave and Cleave (marriage).
  o Fill the Earth and Subdue it.
  o Exercise dominion over all creatures.

We should realize, too, that the curse of God was upon the ground and upon the serpent. He did not curse man, although He did make life more difficult for man.

The Dispensation of Human Government

This is the post-Flood era.

- He was to be fruitful and multiply, to *replenish* the earth.
- Relationships of man and animals were changed, as meat-eating became the norm.
- Man was to require the life of a murderer.
- The following earlier commands still applied:

  o Be fruitful and multiply.
  o Leave and Cleave (marriage).
  o Fill the Earth and Subdue it.
  o Exercise dominion over all creatures.

The Dispensation of Patriarchialism

This is the period beginning with Abram and continuing to the Mosaic Law.

- Man was to be arranged in families or tribes, governed by a patriarch.
- Abram was to be the first patriarch of a people who would ultimately 'spawn' Messiah.
- The following earlier commands still applied:

o   Be fruitful and multiply.
o   Leave and Cleave (marriage.)
o   Fill the Earth and Subdue it.
o   Exercise dominion over all creatures.
o   Human Government was to be in the hands of the patriarch for his tribe.

The Dispensation of Law

This is the period of the Mosaic Law, when God deals primarily with Israel.

- The people of Israel were formed out of slavery in Egypt, redeemed by God, and brought into a new land which was to be theirs. The Mosaic Law was given, to serve as a constitution for the new nation, with very specific regulations in the areas of government, society, economics, and religion. It was a complete, concise compact for the nation. All was centered on their relationship and fellowship with God.
- The following earlier commands still applied:

    o   Be fruitful and multiply.
    o   Leave and Cleave (marriage).

- The earlier commands regarding the control of the whole earth were postponed until the Millennial age.

The Dispensation of the Church

Once again, God developed a whole new way of functioning with a whole new people. These were to be citizens of heaven, not of this earth. They included both Jew and non-Jew, without distinction. The laws of God were to be internalized for them, and dealt with their societal and religious behavior and perspectives, not as a political and economic organization.

- The following earlier commands still applied:

    o   Be fruitful and multiply.
    o   Leave and Cleave (marriage).

- The earlier commands regarding the control of the whole earth were postponed until the Millennial age.
- Human government was in the hands of the secular rulers, not the Church [**Romans 13:1-7; 1 Timothy 2:2**].

The Dispensation of the Millennial or Messianic Kingdom

As we will discuss later in detail, this is a 1000-year reign of Messiah on this Earth, with a redeemed Israel as the centerpiece, and the Church with Messiah, whether in heaven or on earth. The Church is not a part of the Millennial Kingdom, which is made up of human beings and resurrected Old Testament saints.

- Those humans who survived the Tribulation and the Judgments of Christ [**Ezekiel 20:33-38; Matthew 25:31-46**] will continue in the Millennial Kingdom, marrying, bearing children, working, etc.
- Human government will be centered in Messiah, with kings and princes (including David, as we have seen) ruling under Him.
- Man again would have dominion over an earth that would be much like that of the Garden of Eden.
- The following earlier commands still applied:

  o   Be fruitful and multiply.
  o   Leave and Cleave (marriage).

Notice that there is a certain continuity in every dispensation. There is no sharp break or dichotomy. Some of the original commands continued to be in force, while others were modified somewhat from dispensation to dispensation.

One may logically ask, "Why does God work in so many different ways at different times?" Remember two vital points:

1. Jesus Christ is the central, unifying force in each dispensation, whether the individuals could have known of Him or not. He is the Unity that God the Father has chosen to bring these disparate groups and eras together.
2. God is a God of order and reason, and therefore has a definite purpose in all this, though He has not revealed all to us.

With this in mind, let me suggest a possible scenario that may be God's purpose. It is my speculation, but it may prove helpful.

In every dispensation, Man is given instructions and direction by God for that dispensation. Each is **designed to show man the impossibility of living a holy human life apart from God's rule and guidance.**

DISPENSATION OF INNOCENCE

Man might say to God, "Now that I have had fellowship with You, and have seen the bounty of Your grace, and have only one negative command to be concerned with, You can be sure that I will be faithful." But, of course, Adam had all that and failed to be faithful.

DISPENSATION OF CONSCIENCE

Man might say to God, "Now, at least, I have a knowledge of right and wrong, apart from your express commands. Therefore, I can live responsibly and faithfully, relying on my own **conscience**." Man failed that test miserably.

DISPENSATION OF HUMAN GOVERNMENT

Man might say to God, "Well, now I have specific authority and responsibility for governing myself and mine. Therefore, I can live responsibly and faithfully, relying on my own **conscience and** my authority to exercise the "ultimate" punishment, **capital punishment**." Man failed.

DISPENSATION OF PATRIARCHS

Man might say to God, "Now I have a conscience, authority over life and death, AND I have the wisdom of my **patriarch** to make all this work well." It didn't.

DISPENSATION OF LAW

Man might say to God, "Now, at last, we're getting somewhere. Granted, my conscience, my human government, and my patriarchal system didn't work to enable me to live a godly life—but now, with a specific set of instructions from you that embraces all areas of life and with a nation that is united under You—We can surely live a holy life." They failed miserably.

DISPENSATION OF THE CHURCH

Man might say to God, "Now, with a conscience, human government, with the experience of the Patriarchs and the Law, with the revelation of Christ, the new birth, the indwelling of the Holy Spirit, and the spiritual community of believers who are directed to look at things above, not on things of the earth, surely the **church**, at least, will live a godly and holy existence." We haven't.

DISPENSATION OF THE MILLENNIAL KINGDOM

Man might say to God, "Finally, with the **ruling presence of Christ**, with only believers in the kingdom, with the assistance of resurrected Old Testament saints, with the aid of the glorified Church, with the immediate punishment by Christ of rebellion, and with the devil ensconced in the abyss, surely man will live in a holy fashion and will be ever faithful." But, in fact, when Satan is freed for a time, some of the children and grandchildren of those believers will run to his banner, despite having had the advantages noted above.

To sum up, the features and the failures in each dispensation effectively wipe away any notion on the part of man that he can function on his own. These are powerful proofs that **demolish any idea of man being autonomous**. Every man must have a new heart, a new world, and a new spirit—this will be the case when heavenly Jerusalem comes down and the new heavens and new earth come into being.

These destroy every argument of man and leave us totally dependent on God for godly living. And that's a powerful lesson for those today who think the Church will make this old world better. Man needs the kind of relationship Adam originally had, plus a clear recognition of his own inability to do right on his own.

CHAPTER 8

"Give Us a Timetable, Lord"

In this chapter we will summarize the events surrounding the first coming of Messiah, to better prepare us for consideration of the prophecies concerning His second coming.

HIS COMING

During the latter part of the reign of the hated King Herod, the people were hopeful for someone, anyone, but especially the promised Messiah, to come and rescue them from Herod and from his Roman masters. Some did come, preaching rebellion and uprising, but nothing came of them, as they were quickly crushed under the Roman heel. Still, the promise of a victorious Messiah was ever there, and the people, with no other hope before them, longed for His coming.

When Jesus did arrive on the scene, many believed in Him and turned to Him, in the earlier stages of His public ministry. The Gospel writers authenticated His right to be called the Messiah, the Anointed One, through His two-fold genealogies.

Matthew traced Christ's origins back to Abraham, through Isaac, Jacob, and Judah, and ultimately through David and Solomon. This lineage was the authoritative line of kingship, through David. This poses a problem.

For Jeconiah (also known as Jehoiachin or Coniah), a legitimate son of the Davidic line, was accursed by God in the days just before the seventy year captivity. Jehoiachin ruled only some three months on the throne before being taken into captivity by Nebuchadnezzar and the Babylonians. Yet in that brief reign, he managed to incur a curse from God on his progeny. Jeremiah puts this succinctly in [**Jeremiah. 22:24-30**]:

> "'As I live', says the Lord, 'though Coniah the son of Jehoiakim, king of Judah, were the signet on My right hand, yet would I pluck him off; and I will give you into the hand of those who seek your life, and into the hand of Nebuchadnezzar king of Babylon and the hand of the Chaldeans. So I will cast you out, and your mother who bore you, into another country where you were not born; and there you shall die. But to the land to which they desire to return, there they shall not return.
>
> "'Is this man Coniah a despised, broken idol—a vessel in which is no pleasure? Why are they cast out, he and his descendants, and cast into a land which they do not know? O earth, earth, earth, hear the Word of the Lord!' Thus says the Lord: '*Write this man down as childless*, a man who shall not prosper in his days; for *none of his descendants shall prosper, sitting on the throne of David, and ruling anymore in Judah.*'" [italics added]

Hardly a powerful or proud recommendation for the Messiah who was to be king of Israel! Yet this genealogy is that which traces the authoritative line of kingship from David. How are we to understand this?

The answer is found in the last part of the genealogy. In [**Matthew 1:16**]: "And Jacob begat Joseph the husband of Mary, of whom (the *feminine form*, speaking of Mary) was born Jesus who is called Christ." This is the genealogy of Joseph, who was the presumed father of Jesus. Joseph was of the lineage of David, and could trace his roots back through the kingly line. Therefore, as the presumed son of Joseph, Jesus could claim kingly connection with David and Solomon. But, since He was not of the **blood** line of Joseph, He was not subject to the curse of Coniah [**Jeremiah 22:30**].

In the Gospel of Luke, we have a differing genealogy of Jesus, that of His mother, Mary. In this genealogy [**Luke 3:23-38**], Jesus' line is traced (in reverse) back to Adam, again through Abraham, Isaac, and Jacob, and continuing through David. But, at this point there is a remarkable change (verse 31). His lineage here is NOT traced through Solomon or any of the other kings of Judah, but through *another son of David, Nathan*, who was not in the kingly line. Coniah is bypassed altogether in this account. To make matters even clearer, this genealogy begins with a remarkable statement (verse 23):

"Now Jesus Himself began His ministry at about thirty years of age, being (as was supposed) the son of Joseph . . ."

This was not the genealogy of Joseph. It is quite different from that of Matthew. Rather, this is the genealogy of Mary, and traces the blood line of Jesus through her back to *Nathan* and David.

The upshot is that Jesus had a two-fold claim on His relationship to David:

1. Officially, through His presumed father, Joseph, He had the **legal right** to the crown of David.
2. Actually, through His genuine mother, Mary, He had the **blood lineage** traced back to David, to whom the promise of an eternal successor on the throne would come

Upon His birth, through the work of the Holy Spirit, some immediately some knew that He was the promised Messiah. People like Zacharias and Elizabeth, Simeon, and Anna, for example, as well as Mary herself, and, probably, Joseph, realized something of His uniqueness **[Luke 2:19-38]**. However, most would not know of Him in this regard until His presentation of Himself, beginning with His baptism by John the Baptist.

HIS PRESENTATION

Baptism of the type practiced by John the Baptist, was not commonplace in Judah. Ceremonial washings and cleansings were common, but the idea that a Jew was NOT basically clean and acceptable to God was an incredible idea. That John immersed the whole person was unique and hard to accept by most devout Jews, for this implied the necessity of a total cleansing.This was absurd for a people who were very special to God, as they saw it.

Coupled with that strange idea was John's practice of proclaiming the need of a personal repentance on the part of Jews. Again, this seemed to be a bit much to Jews accustomed to thinking of themselves as servants of the One True God. His proclamation of the need for repentance, coupled with the symbolism of the baptismal immersion, brought many enemies, particularly among the religious leaders of the Jews.

Then Jesus Himself, a cousin of John, came publicly to John, requesting baptism. John was appalled, for He believed this Person was, in fact, the Messiah, and clearly in no need of repentance or of baptism. But Jesus insisted, for in this act He formally identified Himself with a nation in great need of repentance and cleansing. And God the Father used this experience to affirm to John that this was the promised Messiah.

We should note here that the basic idea of baptism is that of **identification.** It is not designed to be a church rite, *per se*, nor is it a function of the amount of water used. John immersed to symbolize the need for a **total** repentance and a **total** cleansing. Because of the various practices of the Church over the centuries, we've become somewhat confused about Baptism.

Let us point out what biblical baptism is not:

1. It is not properly a rite of entering the true Church. One does not become a Christian and a member of the Body of Christ by water baptism, but by Spirit Baptism [**1 Corinthians 12:13**]. Only one who has already been born-again is to be baptized. But, when one has been born-again, he or she is *already* a member of the true Church, the body of Christ, before any baptism. So, baptism, properly understood, is an act of **Identification**.

2. It is not a means of acquiring salvation, for that is strictly a matter of faith in Jesus Christ and His finished work on the cross [**1 Peter 3:21**].

3. It does not wash away any sins [**1 Peter 3:21**].

4. The amount of water is not at issue in baptism, (Still, in my view, the normal mode of baptism is full immersion, as the best example of being entirely saved by Jesus Christ, and of illustrating our co-death, co-burial, and co-resurrection with Him).

5. Baptism is not for infants, or for children who are baptized because they are children of believers. Baptism requires repentance (a change of identity and allegiance), and that requires knowledge and judgment. Children certainly may and should be baptized when they have, in fact, trusted Jesus Christ for their personal salvation, but not before.

On the other hand, baptism does signify **identification**:

1. In [**1 Corinthians 10:2**], the term is used to signify the **identification** of the departing Israelites with Moses. Clearly, here there was NO water applied, as every Israelite crossed over on DRY land.

2. As mentioned above, in [**1 Corinthians 12:13**], the term is used to signify **identification** as members of the Body of Christ, through placement by the Holy Spirit, not by an individual's unilateral decision.

3. A Christian is to be baptized as a public expression of having placed faith and reliance in the Person and Work of the Lord Jesus Christ.

4. When Jesus was baptized, it was not due to His personal need for repentance, but to **identify** Himself with His people who were in need of repentance.

He publicly presented Himself in ministry following the imprisonment of John the Baptist, at about age thirty-four. He proclaimed the "Gospel of the Kingdom" (not the Gospel of Grace proclaimed today). He performed the signs and miracles expected of Messiah: healings, raising the dead, forgiving sins, supplying provisions, protecting from natural dangers, and the like. Many thought of Him as the promised Messiah. He formally presented Himself at the time we call "Palm Sunday", when He entered Jerusalem for the Passover, riding on the foal of an ass, in fulfillment of the prophecy of Zechariah [**Zechariah. 9:9**].

HIS REJECTION

"He came to His own, and His own did not receive Him." [**John 1:11**].

After a brief, tumultous welcome from the multitudes of Jewish pilgrims from many lands, who were gathered in Jerusalem for the Passover feast, Jesus' popularity quickly waned. Jerusalem, a large city, was swelled to perhaps a million or more for this great feast time, one of the three feasts required of all Jewish males over age twelve. Jesus was certainly a subject of intense scrutiny and discussion. The air was electric with tension as an impending, inevitable confrontation between Jesus and His followers and official Judaism loomed.

Many of that official religious leadership were scorned and even hated by the multitudes, for their venality and hypocrisy. Still, they were the official keepers of the Law, and, as such, were grudgingly given respect. But a challenge to their authority by One who had such impressive credentials of healings, miracle workings, unique and powerful teaching was applauded and enthusiastically received by many in the crowds.

The Pharisees, Sadduccees, Scribes, Priests and the High Priest joined forces in an unusual alliance to thwart this interloper who threatened their authority and power. They worked the crowds during that week, arguing and convincing people of their assessment of Jesus. When it became clear to the people that this Jesus had no intention of seizing power and confronting the hated Roman occupiers, their initial enthusiasm quickly dissipated. And, the tide turned!

Finally, the High Priests (there was one in nominal authority, but another behind him with real authority), felt strong enough to publicly challenge the Nazarene, and had Him arrested and brought before a hastily-convened Sanhedrin. He was quickly convicted and condemned, and then they took Him before Pilate. They demanded that Pilate have Jesus executed as an enemy of the State (Rome). The same crowd that earlier had hailed Him as their coming King now cried loudly for Jesus' death. The religious leaders, who hated Rome with a passion, now solemnly and loudly declared, "We have no king but Caesar". What a change!

After much maneuvering and hesitation, Pilate finally gave up and consented to Jesus' execution. He was then scourged and humiliated and nailed to a cross as a common criminal. He died on the cross, was taken down and buried in a new tomb, which was then sealed with a huge stone and guards were placed before it. The remnant who still believed in Jesus as the Messiah were crushed. They scattered in grief and fear.

HIS RESURRECTION AND ASCENSION

On the third day, a Sunday, the tomb was empty, with the stone rolled away and the guards gone! Soon, the risen Lord Jesus appeared to a number of His amazed followers and demonstrated that He was real, not a ghost of some sort, but with unique powers not possible to a normal body. In the course of forty days, He appeared to more than 500 of His disciples, transforming them from a crushed, despondent group into an excited, hopeful, courageous band.

After some forty days, within the full view of His band of Apostles, He was taken up into Heaven, disappearing in a cloud [Acts. 1:9]. Two men in white apparel (Angels) told the Apostles to expect Him to return to them in like manner. The Apostles returned to Jerusalem and awaited further events. On the Day of Pentecost, the church was created by the power of the Holy Spirit. It is to the formation of this new thing—the Church—that we now turn our direction.

CHAPTER 9

What is this "Church"?

The Church was created on that Day of Pentecost [Acts 2]. This was a new thing, not revealed or prophesied in the Old Testament. Contrary to the views of many Christians, this was not simply a replacement of the Old Testament "church". Israel was never the Church, nor were there any members of the Church prior to that Day of Pentecost.

Even the Apostles were not part of the Church before that day. Every believer from the time of Adam until that Day of Pentecost was a member of the Family of God. Each was saved by God through the finished work of Jesus Christ on the cross at Calvary, but none was a member of the Church, for it did not exist before that Day. It was a new work of God. This does not mean that the Old Testament saints were somehow inferior to those who would populate the Church, but simply that they were of different households of God's family of saved people. Let us now examine why this is so.

The Church began on the Day of Pentecost. We can see this by the following:

- **[Matthew 16:18]** *"And I say to you that you are Peter and on this rock I will build My church, and the gates of Hades shall not prevail against it."*

  o   This signifies to us that the **Church is yet future**, at this point.

- **[1 Corinthians 12:13, 27]** *"For by one Spirit we were all baptized into one body—whether Jews or Greeks, whether slaves or free—and have all* *been made to drink into one Spirit . . . Now you are the body of Christ, and members individually."*

o   This signifies that the **body of Christ** consists of those who were baptized (identified) into that body, with no distinction of either Jew or Gentile. Nowhere in the Old Testament is there even a hint of such a creation.

- **[Acts 11:15]** *"And as I began to speak, the Holy Spirit fell upon them, **as upon us at the beginning.**"* [bold added]

o   This points out that the events of that Day of Pentecost were unique, providing a **beginning.**

- **[Ephesians 1:22-23]** *"And He put all things under His feet, and gave Him to be head over all things to the church, which is His body . . ."*

o   This brings us full circle, **identifying the Church as the Body of Christ**, which **began on the Day of Pentecost.**

But, is it really a fact that the Church is not the New Testament Israel? Well, let's do a little comparison: Note the differences on each point:

Element	Israel	Church
Entry	Physical Birth	Spiritual Birth
Entrance	Circumcision	Profession
Covenant	Mosaic—Temporary	Grace—Permanent
Laws	Tablets—of stone	Tablets of the heart
Makeup	Jews	Jews + Gentiles
Attendance	Obligatory	Voluntary
Giving	Tithes	Voluntary
Sacrifice for Sin	Daily—Annual	Once—Final
Praise God	meats, food, grain	lips & lives
Forgiveness	Annual—temporary	Permanent—Once
Messiah	Looking for Him	Present in us
Holy Spirit	Among the group	In each believer

Temple	Physical—building	In each believer's body
Priesthood	Special group	Every believer a priest
Future	In Land	In Heaven

But, even with that, why is it so important to distinguish them?

1. The Bible clearly does so.
2. If we were merely a 'better' version of Israel, we would:

- Miss the Indwelling presence of the Holy Spirit.
- Miss the fact that we need no interceding priests—we are priests, and have Christ as High Priest.
- Still be obliged to offer material sacrifices, worship in a temple, and bring tithes to the temple.

No, it is a blessed fact that we are NOT the New Testament version of Israel. We don't need priests, temples, rites of initiation or material sacrifices. In fact, the Church is sort of a preview for Israel of what Israel will be like in the Messianic Kingdom, as we shall see later.

This does not mean we are to consider ourselves superior to Israel, or to saved Israelites—just different. Israel as a nation has a very special place in God's heart and is the centerpiece of His work on Earth. He has made very specific promises to Israel. These promises have not yet been fulfilled. But they will be, for they are dependent on God alone. He keeps His promises.

The church was not seen or prophesied in the Old Testament. The New Testament refers to the church as a 'mystery'—that is, something not earlier revealed [Ephesians 3:3-6]. Paul is quite emphatic that the church is a new thing in God's plan. It is not an afterthought or a plan developed in the wake of Israel's failures. It was planned from the beginning of creation but was not revealed earlier.

The church consists of both Jew and Gentile—as one new entity. Every person who has trusted in the Lord Jesus Christ for his or her salvation is a member of the true church, placed there by the Holy Spirit [1 Corinthians 12:13]. This is true, irrespective of any church membership. Though there are Jewish congregations and Gentile congregations, there is in fact no difference. All are part of the one church. No Gentile believer should consider himself superior to a Jewish believer, and no Jewish believer should think he is better than a Gentile believer. We are one in Christ Jesus.

As noted earlier, the church is completed at the Rapture. Its members are removed from the earth prior to the Tribulation, which is a time of God's Wrath. We are not to experience His wrath [**1 Thessalonians 5:9**]. The church is taken to heaven for the marriage feast of the Lamb and to await the consummation of the Tribulation. The church will then be continually wherever Christ is.

We will speak more of the Marriage Feast of the Lamb later, but think about this: If the church consists of all believers of all time, who, then, is invited to be guests at the marriage feast—unbelievers? [**Revelation 19:8-9; Mattthew 22:8-14**].

All believers of all time are saved in the same way—by the finished sacrificial work of the Lord Jesus Christ on the cross. And each one is an indelible part of the Family of God.

But only those saved since Pentecost and prior to the Rapture are part of the church, the Body of Christ. As we saw in the portion on dispensations, there are a number of different features involved in the management of the different groups.

To argue that every Old Testament saint knew of the finished work of Christ is nonsense. In each era, the saint responded in obedience to the revelation that God had given up to that point, Each saint knew God would have to make him or her clean, but they did not know how He would do it. Each one trusted in the mercy and grace of God to be accepted by Him.

The Church is not an interlude, an afterthought, or an accident, but an important part of the entire glorious program of God for mankind.

Now, we will explore the events of the **Day of The Lord.**

CHAPTER 10

"What's This Day of the Lord"?

The **"Day of the Lord"** is a constantly recurring theme in the Old Testament Prophets and continues in the New Testament. There is room for debate as to the beginning and the end of this time frame, but one thing is certain—basically, it is a time of terrible judgment, on Israel and on the Gentile nations.

In examining the **"Day of the Lord"** passages, keep in mind several things:

1. Sometimes, there is a near and a far view in the Old Testament prophets' writings. That is, there is a mixing of a soon-to-occur event with an event that would occur much later, well beyond the hearers' timeframe. The prophets often used near-term events as a prelude or a germinal description of events far beyond their lifetime. This is often the case with the **"Day of the Lord"** passages. Therefore, one needs to examine them closely for context and in light of what we now know, centuries later, of the events indicated.

2. A quite common phrase that usually denotes the **"Day of the Lord"** is the phrase "in that day". This does not always refer to the end-times **"Day of the Lord",** but often does so.

3. Most often, the term **"Day of the Lord"** deals with end-times events. Occasionally, as in the days of the Babylonian Captivity, there is a use of those events to serve as a precursor to the true end-time **"Day of the Lord"** events.

4. The key to correctly identifying a passage as one referring to the end-times **"Day of the Lord"** is whether or not the prescribed events or conditions have yet come to pass. If we believe that the Bible is God's Word, and therefore true and trustworthy, we cannot brush off such passages as "essentially fulfilled" or "spiritually fulfilled". When we can take a passage literally, we should not seek to "spiritualize" it or treat it as allegorical.

5. We need to accurately understand the events of history subsequent to the writer's time, in order to accurately interpret a passage. Whenever logical, we should take the Scripture literally. When the passage is clearly allegorical or symbolic, we should take it so. But, if it can be understood in its normal wording, we should take it literally. For example, when Jesus said "I am the door", one would never think He was describing Himself as a literal, physical door. This is obviously metaphorical. But, when we are told that, "Therefore, if anyone is in Christ, he is a new creation . . ." [**2 Corinthians 5:17a**], we should take that literally. We assume literal interpretation unless it is clearly metaphorical.

There are many passages clearly dealing with the **Day of the Lord** as an end-time event. Here are a few. There is a more complete list in Appendix 1:

- *"For the day of the Lord of hosts shall come upon everything proud and lofty. Upon everything lifted up; and it shall be brought low"* [Isaiah 2:12].
- *"Wail, for the day of the Lord is at hand! It will come as destruction from the Almighty"* [Isaiah 13:6].
- *"Behold, the day of the Lord comes, cruel, with both wrath and fierce anger, to lay the land desolate; and He will destroy its sinners from it"* [Isaiah 13:9].
- *"For this is the day of the Lord God of hosts, a day of vengeance, that He may avenge Himself on His adversaries. The sword shall devour; it shall be satiated and made drunk with their blood; for the Lord God of hosts has a sacrifice in the north country by the river Euphrates"* [Jeremiah 46:10].
- *"You have not gone up into the gaps to build a wall for the house of Israel to stand in battle on the day of the Lord"* [Ezekiel 13:5].
- *"For the day is near, even the day of the Lord is near; it will be a day of clouds, the time of the Gentiles"* [Ezekiel 30:3].
- *"Alas for the day! For the day of the Lord is at hand; it shall come as destruction from the Almighty"* [Joel 1:15].

- *"Blow the trumpet in Zion, and sound an alarm in My holy mountain! Let all the inhabitants of the land tremble; for the day of the Lord is coming, for it is at hand"* [**Joel 2:1**].
- *"The Lord gives voice before His army, for His camp is very great; for strong is the One who executes His word. For the day of the Lord is great and very terrible; who can endure it?"* [**Joel 2:11**].
- *"The sun shall be turned into darkness, and the moon into blood, before the coming of the great and awesome day of the Lord"* [**Joel 2:31**].
- *"Multitudes, multitudes in the valley of decision! For the day of the Lord is near in the valley of decision"* [**Joel 3:14**].
- *"Woe to you who desire the day of the Lord! For what good is the day of the Lord to you? It will be darkness, and not light"* [**Amos 5:18**].
- *"Is not the day of the Lord darkness, and not light? Is it not very dark, with no brightness in it?"* [**Amos 5:20**].
- *"For the day of the Lord upon all nations is near; as you have done, it shall be done to you; your reprisal shall return upon your own head"* [**Obadiah 15**].
- *"Be silent in the presence of the Lord God; for the day of the Lord is at hand, for the Lord has prepared a sacrifice; He has invited His guests"* [**Zephaniah 1:7**].
- *"The great day of the Lord is near; it is near and hastens quickly. The noise of the day of the Lord is bitter; there the mighty men shall cry out"* [**Zephaniah 1:14**].
- *"Behold, the day of the Lord is coming, and your spoil will be divided in your midst"* [**Zechariah 14:1**].
- *"Behold, I will send you Elijah the prophet before the coming of the great and dreadful day of the Lord"* [**Malachi 4:5**].
- *"The sun shall be turned into darkness, and the moon into blood, before the coming of the great and awesome day of the Lord"* [**Acts 2:20**].
- *"For you yourselves know perfectly that the day of the Lord so comes as a thief in the night"* [**1 Thessalonians 5:2**].
- *"But the day of the Lord will come as a thief in the night, in which the heavens will pass away with a great noise, and the elements will melt with fervent heat; both the earth and the works that are in it will be burned up"* [**2 Peter 3:10**].
- *" . . . looking for and hastening the coming of the day of God, because of which the heavens will be dissolved being on fire, and the elements will melt with fervent heat"* [**2 Peter 3:12**].

From these verses and others, we can glean certain information:

1. The **Day of the Lord** could not be the Babylonian captivity, as many passages written subsequent to that period refer to it as future.
2. The **Day of the Lord** is a time of terrible judgment by God; it is not a delightful thing.
3. The **Day of the Lord** is not just for the Jews, but for Gentiles also.
4. The **Day of the Lord** did not occur during the days of the early church, as Acts and Second Peter (two later New Testament Epistles) speak of it as yet future.
5. The **Day of the Lord** comes suddenly and unexpectedly.
6. The **Day of the Lord** is evidently an extended period of time.
7. The **Day of the Lord** is in two stages—one prior to the return of the Lord Jesus, and the other subsequent to His earthly kingdom. For, clearly, the heavens and earth don't melt prior to His messianic earthly kingdom. Only by denying the many passages that speak of that earthly kingdom could one force the **Day of the Lord** into one solitary event, as some suggest, using Second Peter as their supporting Scripture.
8. The **Day of the Lord** is not the event of the defeat of the Jews and the destruction of the Temple in A.D. 70.
9. In no logical way could the **Day of the Lord** be seen as a blessed or happily anticipated time by the New Testament saints—the Church.

The **Day of the Lord** is a very important part of God's revelation to man. It carries with it the same type of chill that a reading of the Seal, Trumpet and Bowl judgments of Revelation does. It is a time of unprecedented trouble. This is aptly captured by the Lord Jesus Himself in a reference to events of the **Day of the Lord,** [**Matthew 24:21ff**].

The Lord Jesus describes this as *"For then there will be great tribulation, such as has not been since the beginning of the world until this time, no, nor ever shall be."* [**Matthew 24:21**]

It is the events and sequence of the **Day of the Lord** that we will be trying to understand and set in a reasonable order. For, though there is a super-abundance of Scripture referring to that time, it is not given in a sequential, cohesive pattern. We must study, examine, and correlate.

Still, a Christian might ask, "Why should we, as Christians, study this so carefully, if we are not subject to its events?" There are a number of reasons why we should study it, and we dare not avoid considering it carefully.

1. It does, after all, consume a major portion of Scripture, both Old Testament and New Testament.
2. Obviously, it is there for a reason; and Christians are called again and again to consider it.
3. One really cannot satisfactorily explain the book of the Revelation without considering the mass of teaching about the **Day of the Lord.**
4. There are many things written in both Testaments that may not concern us experientially, but are nonetheless very important. For one instance, the future of Satan. Another would be the future of the nation Israel.

So, study it we shall, and in the process I'm confident you will begin to see the significance and importance of it all. For one thing, in my view, the prophesied future of the nation of Israel is the best possible assurance that my salvation is safe and secure. For another, the very character and veracity of God is at stake in all this.

Let us now go on to consider the teaching and validity of the taking away of the church prior to the beginning of the **Day of the Lord**—the event we call the "Rapture".

CHAPTER 11

"What is the Rapture?" (Part 1)

T HE RAPTURE IS the event that will trigger the **Day of the Lord**. It is absolutely vital to Christians, as it is the event that completes the Church, the Body of Christ.

There are several major points we need to make before we begin our detailed study.

- There are no known events that *must* transpire before the Rapture. In other words, it could occur at any time.
- The Day of Pentecost [**Acts 2**] begins the formation of the Church, the Body of Christ. The Rapture completes that formation. Although people are saved subsequent to the Rapture, they are not part of the Body of Christ, His Bride. There will be other households in God's Kingdom, all saved by the finished work of Christ on the cross at Calvary.
- The Rapture must occur sometime before the **Day of the Lord** is ushered in, for the Church is specifically promised they will be spared from the time of the Lord's wrath [**1 Thessalonians 5:9**].
- The Rapture will include each and every living true Christian. These will receive transformed bodies [**1 Corinthians 15:50-57**].
- The Rapture will be the time for the bodily resurrection of those who "sleep in Jesus"; i.e., the saints who have died since the formation of the Church at Pentecost [**1 Thessalonians 4:13-18**]. Conversely, the Old Testament Jewish saints are promised a bodily resurrection at the end of the Great Tribulation [**Daniel 12:1-2**].

- The Rapture is limited to the members of the Body of Christ [1 Thessalonians 4:14-15].

The major text which teaches the fact of the Rapture is [1 Thessalonians 4:13-18]. Let's now look at that passage in some detail. The context is set in the entire First Epistle to the Thessalonians, and is important to understand this context.

This is Paul's first canonical writing and is written to reassure members of the Church concerning the return of the Lord Jesus. Many believing scholars date this in early A.D. 51, some 18 or so years subsequent to the Day of Pentecost. Paul describes his purpose and theme in each chapter of 1 Thessalonians:

> 1:10 *"and to wait for His Son from heaven, whom He raised from the dead, even Jesus who delivers us from the wrath to come."*
>
> 2:19 *"For what is our hope, or joy, or crown of rejoicing? Is it not even you in the presence of our Lord Jesus Christ at His coming?"*
>
> 3:13 *"so that He may establish your hearts blameless in holiness before our God and Father at the coming of our Lord Jesus Christ with all His saints."*
>
> 4:17 *"Then we who are alive and remain shall be caught up together with them in the clouds to meet the Lord in the air. And thus we shall always be with the Lord."*
>
> 5:23 *"Now may the God of peace Himself sanctify you completely; and may your whole spirit, soul, and body be preserved blameless at the coming of our Lord Jesus Christ."*

Why this emphasis on the Lord's return for His Church? Simply to reassure and comfort the Christians. Almost two decades have passed and—no return. Could the Lord have changed His mind? What about the Christians who have died already? A multitude of such questions would have arisen by this time. It is to answer these that Paul writes both of his Thessalonian epistles.

But the teaching of the fourth chapter of First Thessalonians is about more than the mere assurance of the return of the Lord Jesus. It is intended to provide real comfort and assurance to the saints regarding not only their own future with Christ, but also the situation for departed fellow-believers. Have those Christians who have already died somehow missed out on the bodily resurrection, since Christ has not yet returned? If I, as a Christian, should die before He returns, will I fail to get a resurrection body? Or, must I wait until some unspecified time for my resurrection body? Paul's answer is quite clear, and quite comforting.

He begins in verse 13 of Chapter four, thus:

> *4:13) "But I do not want you to be ignorant, brethren, concerning those who have fallen asleep, lest you sorrow as others who have no hope."*

Paul says this is not something about which we should know nothing. If it were, we would be in a condition similar to non-believers, who have no hope. Clearly, the teaching he presents is something that is central to Christian belief and is the basis for great comfort.

> *4:14) "For if we believe that Jesus died and rose again, even so God will bring with Him those who sleep in Jesus."*

Assuredly, Christians believe in and should count on their resurrection, since Jesus Himself has been bodily resurrected, Paul says. The term "those who sleep in Jesus" is a euphemism for the physical death of *Christians* (as distinguished from believers who died prior to Pentecost.)

Note that it is restricted to those who have known directly of the saving work of Jesus Christ and have trusted specifically in Him. This would exclude saints such as David, for example, who knew something of Messiah (Christ), but nothing of "Jesus". Indeed, if this were to include saints of all ages, it would directly contradict [**Daniel 12:1-2**]. Paul is speaking only to Christians and only about Christians.

Notice also that Paul says "God will bring with Him", saying that God Himself is coming. But in the other passages we noted in this epistle, it is the Son [**1 Thessalonians 1:10**], Jesus [**1 Thessalonians 1:10**], the Lord Jesus Christ [**1 Thessalonians 2:19; 3:13; and 5:23**] who is coming. This is one of many clear teachings that Jesus is the Messiah. He is the Lord. He is God.

Finally, this tells us that the Christian saints who have died are not "moldering" in the ground (though their bodies are), but are at this moment with God in heaven. Paul later makes that clear in [**2 Corinthians 5:6,8**], where he teaches that "to be absent from the body . . . [is] to be present with the Lord."

But, since they have not been bodily resurrected, this refers to their soul and spirit [**1 Thessalonians 5:23**]. He will bring the souls and spirits of the dead in Christ with Him from heaven.

What can we expect, if this is to be the case? He continues to bring out what will happen and how.

> *4:15) "For this we say to you by the word of the Lord, that we who are alive and remain until the coming of the Lord will by no means precede those who are asleep."*

Once again, Paul uses a euphemism, "those who are asleep" to signify physical death. Those coming with the Lord are not asleep, but their physical bodies are. And this event is not some speculation on Paul's part, but is by the "word of the Lord".

Paul identifies two groups of Christians to be involved at Christ's coming; "we who are alive and remain" and "those who are asleep." Neither group has resurrection bodies at this point.

Paul makes a further statement that our being alive on planet earth at this event does not mean we are better off or more privileged than those Christians who have already died. Instead, he assure the living Christians that these departed Christians will be the first to receive their new bodies. In this way, he reassures the Thessalonian Christians that their departed loved ones will miss out on absolutely nothing. Indeed, they have already spent their time apart from their bodies with the Lord in heaven. That's real comfort indeed.

Just how will this all come together and when?

> *4:16) "For the Lord Himself will descend from heaven with a shout, with the voice of an archangel, and with the trumpet of God. And the dead in Christ will rise first."*

This will begin to happen when the Lord descends from heaven, with a cry of the Victor. This could not mean, as some insist, that this is the time prophesied in [Zechariah 14:3-4] (that is, at the end of the Great Tribulation). The conditions and anticipations here described are entirely different from that description of the Lord's coming to judge the nations. Also, the following verses show that the Lord is not descending to earth, but will meet the saints of the Church "in the air". Why in the air? Because it occurs before He returns to earth as Conqueror and Judge.

Notice again that he limits the bodily resurrection to "the dead in Christ". If he had not done so, we might have assumed that [Daniel 12:1-2] might also apply at this time. This teaching is not for all of God's people of all time who have died, but is limited to the Church saints.

Since the spirits and souls of these saints have been in heaven and are now in company with the Lord as He descends, this can only mean that their new bodies are rising from the grave to be reunited with the new spirit nature and the cleansed souls of the dead in Christ.

Man was made body, soul, and spirit at the creation, and he will be made complete again when his body is resurrected. The resurrection of the bodies of those in Christ will precede other resurrections as a demonstration of 'first-fruits' of those bought by Christ.

But, what about those who are alive and remain at this event? Will we have to suddenly keel over and die in order to receive our resurrection bodies?

> 4:17) *"Then we who are alive and remain shall be caught up together with them in the clouds to meet the Lord in the air. And thus we shall always be with the Lord."*

Our bodies will be transformed. There is no suggestion of physical death here. Paul later explains just how that will happen [**1 Corinthians 15:51-54**]. We shall be changed or transformed. In that passage, Paul teaches this as he explains the nature of the resurrection body.

None of this takes place on the earth. Nowhere does it suggest that the Lord actually comes to the earth; quite the contrary. The meeting takes place "in the air"; we are "caught up together with them". This is quite unlike the many passages that speak of the Lord's coming to earth physically to rule and reign. Mistaken views of some Christians concerning this occur in part because they do not recognize the Church as a distinct household of God that does NOT encompass saints of all ages and eras.

> 4:18) *"Therefore comfort one another with these words."*

This teaching of the Rapture is designed to be a message of comfort specifically for the Church. It is written to reassure us that saints who die before the Rapture will not be somehow excluded or overlooked. We are also reassured that we will meet the Lord **before** He pours out His Wrath on the world. Every true believer will be taken up, whether or not he or she believed in the doctrine of the Rapture.

It would be small comfort indeed for "those who are alive and remain" if they were believers who would have to endure an extended period of the 'great and terrible Wrath of God', as the Great Tribulation is described.

It certainly would not be telling them anything new, for of course the saints left alive on the earth at the end of the Tribulation will be with the Lord. This makes real sense only when one sees that this is a special event to remove the Church from Earth, since the Church is not under the Wrath of God.

If the Church were to experience the Wrath of God, the idea that some would survive and those who did not would be resurrected, might be a basis for gratitude and relief, but hardly a basis for comfort. In such a case, a better basis for comfort would be an assurance that a believer would *die prior* to the Great Tribulation. Then, I would be one of those in heaven who returns with the Lord. Those who insist this passage refers to the end of the Tribulation must surely wear severely-tinted rose-colored glasses.

In Chapter five of First Thessalonians, as well as in Second Thessalonians, Paul gives further assurance that this event will precede the Great Tribulation. We will now turn our attention to the basis for this assurance.

CHAPTER 12

"Tell Me More About the Rapture" (Part 2)

In the previous chapter, we pointed out several things that must be true relative to the event we call the "Rapture." These points included:

- There are no known events that must transpire before the Rapture. In other words, it could occur at any time.
- The Rapture must occur sometime before the **Day of the Lord** is ushered in, for the Church is specifically promised they will be spared from the time of the execution of the Lord's wrath.
- The Rapture will encompass each and every living Christian. These will receive transformed bodies.
- The Rapture will be the time for the bodily resurrection of every one who "sleeps in Jesus"; i.e., the saints who have died since the formation of the Church at Pentecost. By way of contrast, the Old Testament Jewish saints are promised a bodily resurrection at the end of the Great Tribulation [Daniel 12:1-2].
- The Rapture is limited to the members of the Body of Christ, and to no other saints.

Let's deal with these one at a time, in the light of what we have already seen concerning this Rapture [1 Thessalonians 4:13-18].

There are no known events that **must** transpire before the Rapture. In other words, it could occur at any time. This is known as the doctrine of "Imminency". Some Christians deny this doctrine, saying that many events must occur before the tribulation—among them, the building of the Temple.

If that is the case, then the Christians of that era would have this or other harbingers which would alert them to the impending return. But, that is contrary to Paul's teaching that this will be sudden and surprising. [**1 Thessalonians 5:2**].

But, does not the Temple have to be built before the tribulation? It would be difficult to build it during that time of great destruction. And, if it is built or in process before the tribulation, would not the Church saints see that and know about that?

- Generally, this is often perceived to be the case based on a reading of [**Daniel 9:27**], which says, " . . . *But in the middle of the week he shall bring an end to sacrifice and offering. And on the wing of abominations shall be one who makes desolate, even until the consummation, which is determined, is poured out on the desolate.*"
- This idea is buttressed by [**2 Thessalonians 2:4**], " . . . *so that he (the Man of Sin) sits as God in the temple of God, showing himself that he is God.*"

  o But this does not necessarily mean the Temple of the Jews. It could refer to any place the Great Man might choose to establish for worship of himself.

- The assumption is that there must be a Temple, since there will be "sacrifice and offering" during the time of the tribulation. That is certainly conceivable, but there are some other issues to consider:

  o In order for the temple to exist at this time, several prior events must occur.
  o First, the Al Aqsa Mosque and the Dome of the Rock Mosque must be removed from the temple mount area.
  o This means that either the Muslims would be unable to prevent this from happening, or that they would somehow acquiesce in their destruction. That would be quite a feat, even for the Great Man.
  o Then, within a very short span of time, a suitable temple would have to be rebuilt on this same area.

- o Further, a priestly caste would have to be identified to carry out these sacrifices.
- o Israel (the nation) would desire to re-institute the Mosaic Law and sacrificial system. Currently, only about 10 per cent of the nation of Israel would have much interest in that. The balance of the Israelites are largely secular in their perspective, merely paying lip service (often, quite grudgingly) to the religious practices even of today.
- o If a Temple were to be built, it would surely be destroyed during the terrible events of the last three and one-half years, or in the battle for Jerusalem [**cf. Zechariah 14**].
- o It is striking that no hint of the Temple is found in [**Zechariah 14**], when the destruction of the city is described in detail.

Of course, all that is not impossible, but is most unlikely. However, it is not necessary for the Temple to be rebuilt at this time in order to fulfill the prophecy. (There will be a Temple built following the Return of Christ [**Ezekiel 40-48**]).

It would be entirely possible to have sacrifices and offerings re-instituted with some sort of an altar near the current "wailing wall" (which is part of the foundation wall of Herod's Temple). A small portion of the Temple Mount area could be set aside for this purpose without disturbing either of the two mosques, assuming the Man of Sin could so persuade the Muslims. Israel long had sacrifices and offerings without a Temple, and could do so again. If merely an altar were created, then the minority orthodox Jews could sacrifice without involving all of the nation.

The bottom line is, we simply do not know whether or not a Temple would be rebuilt at that time. It might be, although it need not be. In any event, it does not have to be rebuilt before the Rapture occurs.

The Rapture must occur sometime **before** the **Day of the Lord** is ushered in, for the Church is specifically promised they will be **spared** from the time of the execution of the Lord's wrath. This is clearly indicated in the following passages:

- • [**1 Thessalonians 1:10**] *"and to wait for His Son from heaven, whom He raised from the dead, even Jesus who delivers us from* (Greek: **apo** [from], not **ek** [out of]), *the wrath to come."*
- • [**1 Thessalonians 5:4**] *"But you, brethren, are not in darkness, so that this Day should overtake you as a thief."*

- **[1 Thessalonians 5:9]** *"For God did not appoint* (Greek: **atheto**, from **tithimi**—to place, set, appoint) *us to wrath, but to obtain salvation through our Lord Jesus Christ."*

Evidence that the Church is not on earth during the Great Tribulation is seen in passages like: **[Matthew 24:14-20]**. Clearly, the Church is not in view here, but Israel is. The Church would not be in Jerusalem or Judaea, and would not be concerned with traveling regulations concerning the Sabbath.

The Rapture will be the time for the bodily resurrection of every one of those who "sleep in Jesus". The question again is "who are those who 'sleep in Jesus?" Does this include every saint of every age? Why does Paul not say the "Lord Jesus" or "Christ?"

- In the Epistles, the writers almost always use terms like "Lord Jesus", "Lord Jesus Christ", "Christ Jesus", "Christ", or some similar term, focusing on His Position and/or Title.
- Whenever they use the term "Jesus" without an adjective, they are almost always focusing on His humanity, rather than on His deity or Lordship. The reason is to emphasize the humanity of Christ for a particular purpose.
- In fact, a survey of the Epistles will show that **the use of "Jesus" occurs less than 5 per cent of all the times He is specifically named.** I think that is no accident. Perhaps we today should follow that example and speak more of "The Lord Jesus Christ" or similar, rather than "Jesus", unless we are specifically seeking to emphasize His humanity.
- Thus, here he uses "Jesus" to delineate those who died as believers since Jesus walked the earth. It must be those who have died in Jesus since the "beginning", the formation of the church.
- In fact, the saints of the Old Testament (at least, the Jewish ones) will be bodily resurrected *after* the Tribulation Judgment **[Daniel 12:1-2]**.

The Rapture is limited to the members of the Body of Christ, and to no other saints. Nowhere, prior to the Epistles, is any saint said to be part of the Body of Christ. It is not even mentioned in the Gospels. Furthermore, nowhere in Revelation (beyond Chapter 3) is a believer on earth said to be part of the Body of Christ.

- Peter states in **[Acts 11:15]**, "And as I began to speak, the Holy Spirit fell upon them, as upon us at the *beginning*." [italics added]. What beginning? Clearly, he has the Pentecost of [Acts 2] in mind. What began, then, at that time? The Church, which was not seen in the Old Testament; rather, it was a mystery previously unrevealed. [Ephesians 1:9-10; 3:4-6].

- Nowhere in the Old Testament are the saints assured they will not experience the **Day of the Lord**; quite the contrary [cf. Habakkuk 3]. In the Gospels, Matthew quotes Jesus as stating emphatically that Jewish believers will experience the Tribulation [Matthew 24:13].

The reality is this: The defining issue in interpreting Scripture rests on one's view of the Church; what it is, who it is, and why it is. By this time, it should be evident that Israel is neither the replaced Church nor the original Church. The Church is not a new, improved version of Israel. This false notion has done a great deal of damage, through the centuries, to both Jew and Gentile, and to the Church itself.

So, what is the future of the Church? This is a unique body of believers bound together from the Day of Pentecost until the Day of the Rapture. This group will not undergo the Wrath of God (**Day of the Lord**), but will be taken out of the way, as the restraining influence of the Holy Spirit manifested through the sin-dampening influence of the Church is removed [2 Thessalonians 2:6-7].

The Church will then be "ever with the Lord", Who is in Heaven. Their "citizenship is in Heaven, not on the earth." They are strangers and sojourners on earth, whereas the Jewish saints are advised again and again to focus on the earth, on the land that is theirs.

We know three things for certain:

1) We shall always be with the Lord from the moment of the Rapture and ever after [1 Thessalonians 4:17].
2) We shall, the betrothed to Christ, become the Bride of Christ [Revelation 19:7-9].
3) We shall be with God and Christ in the new heavens and new earth [Revelation 21-22].

With this in mind, let's move on to examine the Tribulation.

CHAPTER 13

Getting the Ball Rolling

The immediate effect of the Rapture is to get the last major hindrance to the Great Man's predominance out of the way. This is described in [2 Thessalonians 2:3-8].

- A "falling away" (apostasia) will precede the return of the Lord, and pave the way for the unopposed pre-eminence of the Great Man.
- The "apostasy" is described in [1 Timothy 4:1-3; 2 Timothy 4:3]. This will increase and expand until the time when the Lord comes for His Bride, the Church.
- This "falling away" will be accelerated when that which restrains is taken out of the way. This refers to the restraining influence of the Holy Spirit through the instrumentality of His Church.
- The term translated "what is restraining" in [2 Thessalonians 2:6] has a neuter article, which correlates with the term "Holy Spirit", which is also neuter.
- However, the terms "He who now restrains" is in the masculine gender, indicating personality, which signifies that the Holy Spirit is not just a force, but is a distinct Person. In [Acts 5:1-9], we get a confirmation that the Holy Spirit is a Person, in the recounting of verses 1-4. There we see that Ananias lied to the Holy Spirit. One cannot lie to a "force", but only to a person. We further see there that the Holy Spirit is indeed God ("you have not lied to men but to God").
- The Holy Spirit, acting largely through the Church, has been holding back the affairs and wills of men, keeping them from unrestrained evil.

When the Church is removed, there is no human instrumentality to further restrain man. So he is now free to carry out the lifestyles of a man without God [**Romans 1:24-32**], without brake or interference.

- This does not mean the Holy Spirit is absent from the world. He continues active in the 144,000 and the two Witnesses [**Revelation 11; Revelation 14:1-5**], for example, but the substantial restraining influence He has exerted through the Church is now removed.

- This will then pave the way for the Great Man to carry out his program [**2 Thessalonians 2:9-12**] with virtual impunity. He will develop various explanations for the loss of so many in the Rapture, and the people who remain will eagerly embrace such explanations, so they may continue unimpeded in their unrighteous activities [**2 Thessalonians 2:11-12**].

This is a short chapter, but one that has tremendous significance, and provides necessary details to explain the shift from these times to the cataclysmic **Day of the Lord**.

CHAPTER 14

The Kingdom of Heaven

One of the important, but confusing elements of the New Testament is the idea of the Kingdom of Heaven. This is found only in the Gospel of Matthew, one of the Synoptic Gospels. The Gospels of Mark and Luke use the term, "Kingdom of God". However, these are not synonymous terms.

The Kingdom of Heaven is part of the Kingdom of God. The Kingdom of God covers God's rule everywhere and in everything, including Heaven.The "Kingdom of Heaven" is located not in Heaven, but on the earth. It is the promised Kingdom Age prophesied extensively in the Old Testament. It is particularly important for the Jews, but does encompass the Gentile nations in the Kingdom Age.

Many commentators treat these terms as synonymous and thus draw inaccurate conclusions when interpreting the New Testament. This has been particularly prevalent among those groups who do not see Israel as having a distinct future. But it is wrong.

Matthew uses the term because he is writing specifically to the Jews. It is true that Mark and Luke also address the Jewish people, but their primary purpose and focus is to explain the Jews to other groups.

Mark provides a picture of Jesus, the Christ, as a servant king, and focuses on audiences with a Roman background or mindset. Thus, the disctinction would not be of particular importance.

Luke writes for an audience with a Greek education or background, and handles this much as Mark does. Luke draws a picture of Jesus that focuses on Him as the "Son of Man".

Matthew, writing to a basically Jewish audience, emphasizes the Jewish aspect of the Kingdom of God, focusing on Jesus' relationship to the Jews of this era and the era to come. When John the Baptist comes on the scene, he proclaims the "Gospel of the Kingdom", the future Kingdom for David and the Jews on this earth. Likewise, when Jesus begins His earthly ministry, He proclaims the identical "Gospel of the Kingdom", an earthly reign.

How do we know this is so? Whenever this Kingdom of Heaven is noted, the activities and consequences are on earth. For example, the Beatitudes of Matthew five describe a wonderful inheritance for the earth, not for Heaven. In going through the parables, it is clear that it is earth in view, not Heaven. Of course, it is not wrong for either Mark or Luke to use the Kingdom of God in similar events, for the Kingdom of Heaven is indeed an aspect of the Kingdom of God. But, Matthew is particularly addressing the Jewish nation and focuses on their particular interest.

John, in his Gospel, is writing long after the nation of Judea has been dispersed and the Temple destroyed. There is no nation of Judea or Israel to address by his time. His focus is on Jesus as God the Son.

Some insist they are synonymous, regardless, based on a reading of [Matthew 19:23-24], where both the Kingdom of Heaven and the Kingdom of God are seen. The assumption is that verse 24 is merely a repetition of verse 23, with slight variations. But, a close look will show that these statements are distinct, not mirrored. Instead, Jesus is averring that it is hard for a rich man to get into the Kingdom of Heaven (the earthly kingdom), and it is even harder for him to enter the larger, eternal Kingdom of God. Rather than showing commonality, there is an emphasis on their distinction.

I call this "Kingdom of Heaven" the "Messianic Kingdom", or the "Millennial Kingdom" in this book, for that's what it is. It refers to the reign of Christ on this earth for 1000 years. Why is it important to see the distinction? Because God, in Matthew, introduces three distinct eras, related to the Jews.

The first is the Mosaic Law, a system of rules of God has given specifically and exclusively to the Jews, while they are in the land. This is a system of external rules, governing life and conduct in the land.

The second is the Kingdom Age, introduced primarily in Matthew five to seven, buttressed by a number of parables relating to the Kingdom of Heaven. In this Kingdom Age, the primary focus is on Israel in the land, but in a far different condition. The system here involves a set of *internal* rules, much tighter and stronger than the rules of the Mosaic Law. One can readily see this in the teachings of Jesus in this portion of Matthew.

He begins by saying, "The Law says", referring to the law of Moses. Then, in every case, he "tightens up" with a Law that is internalized, and is more demanding than the Mosaic Law.

First, he refers to murder, spelled out in one of the ten commandments. He internalizes this by saying that one can be a "murderer" in his heart.

He does the same thing with adultery, saying that lusting after a woman is effectively adultery.

He tightens the law regarding divorce and remarriage as well, saying that there is no basis for divorce and remarriage.

I have written a small book about this, explaining why the so-called "exception" clause is not an exception clause at all. It's too involved to cover here, but just think of it this way. If Jesus is tightening up on the Mosaic Law in every other instance, why would He be relaxing it here? And, if He does provide an exception, He is easing the penalty, for the prescribed penalty for Adultery is not divorce, but stoning.

But, why would the laws of the new Kingdom Age be tighter and internalized? Because, Satan is bound, all in the Kingdom are believers, and Eden-like qualities of life are everywhere. Plus, the Old Testament saints are resurrected and there for counsel and support. Then, too, Christ will be there, and David will be their king.

Notice that most of the parables speak of the Kingdom Age and conditions. We err when we attribute these to conditions today for Christians. We can learn from them as principles but are mistaken in seeking to make them rules of life for today.

The third era is that of the Church. Late in the Gospel of Matthew, Christ begins to prepare His disciples for the coming Church Age. This, too, is internalized, but *our* citizenship is in Heaven, not on the earth. Our focus is to be on the things above, not the things of this world [Colossians 3:1-4].

We will refer to these distinctions again as we consider the end times.

CHAPTER 15

"We've Got Questions"

To provide sufficient background for the unfolding of the "Great Day", a detailed look at Matthew 24 will be helpful. This passage is called "The Olivet Discourse", Jesus' final counsel to His disciples on the Wednesday of His final week. Jesus provides startling answers to two questions His disciples asked.

Jesus has just finished with a scathing, contentious discussion with the religious leaders in Jerusalem. He now departs the Temple scene and heads for the Mount of Olives, with His disciples in tow. His recent statement to them, as they were leaving still rings in their ears with alarming implications.

He has told them this lovely, revered city is coming under God's judgment. [Matthew 23:37-39]. They are appalled at such an incredible statement. As they are trudging up the hill to the Mount of Olives, they turn and gaze over the beautiful scene once more. Finally, one musters up enough courage to call the Master's attention to this view. [Matthew 24:1-2]. Jesus goes even further, declaring that the Temple and the city will both be utterly destroyed. This judgment was fulfilled in A.D. 70.

Finally, seated in the shade of an ancient olive tree, the bewildered disciples seek to make sense of this. They conclude that Jesus must be referring to the destruction outlined in Zechariah [Zechariah 12:1-6; 14:1-2]. With this in mind, they also recall that it is said there that the Kingdom Age will come in and the Messiah will return to rule. And so, they pose two questions of Jesus.

The first question is: "Tell us, when will these things be?" The second question is more complicated: "And what will be the sign of your coming, and of the end of the age?" [**Matthew 24:3**].

Jesus provides an answer to the first question, giving a full, but sobering answer. He says that a lot of things must happen before all this falls in place. He cites several events that can be expected before the end comes [**Matthew 24:4-7**].

First, he warns that many psudo-Messiahs will come and will prove effectively deceptive. There will be wars and rumors of wars, famines, pestilences, and earthquakes. All these will be just precursors of the approach of the end of the age in which they live. He calls these the "beginning of sorrows" (literally, "the birthpangs") [**Matthew 24:8**].

Second, Jesus indicates that even more disastrous events are to be expected. In these, [**Matthew 24:9-14**], He is thinking beyond that current generation to a more remote time. These events will be to another generation and will come about just before the Great Tribulation develops. There will be tribulation and death for some, and those who follow Jesus will be hated of all nations. There will be defections from the Faith and many will be deceived. Lawlessness (disobedience before God) will increase exponentially, and many who profess Christ will grow cold in their love of Him [**Matthew 24:9-12**]. I believe this describes the events just before the Great Tribulation. He concludes this part with two remarkable statements.

His first is "But he who endures to the end shall be saved." [**Matthew 24:13**]. Who is this and what does it mean? The "end" is the end of the seven-year Tribulation period. The one who "endures" is the believer who manages to remain alive during all that terrible time. Jesus is not speaking here of being "saved" in the sense of being born-again, but simply being saved from death.

His second statement is similar. Just as John the Baptist and Jesus proclaimed "The kingdom is at hand", so in the events directly leading up the the Kingdom Age, this Gospel will again be proclaimed, throughout the world. This will be done primarily through the 144,000 and the two Witnesses.

This is not the Gospel we proclaim today, which is an invitation to turn from sin and become personally related to the Lord Jesus, not to gain land in Israel or anywhere else, but to obtain an eternal salvation. Sometimes, Christian commentators have generated much confusion in equating these different Gospels. This "Gospel of the Kingdom" is the good news that the Kingdom of Heaven has arrived.

As a result of hearing and obeying that Gospel, people will then recognize the error when the Great Man sets himself up as world ruler in Jerusalem. He will demand that every one (especially Jews) must be marked with "666" to be able to eat and live [Matthew 24:15-20].

Thus will begin the "Great Tribulation" [Matthew 24:21]. This will be such a devastating time that no one could physically survive, if God did not cut short the time [Matthew 24:21-22].This Great Tribulation will occur during the last three and one-half years of the seven-year period covered by the Seal, Trumpet, and Bowl Judgments. I believe the Trumpet Judgments and the Bowl Judgments will both occur very near the end of the last three and one-half years.

Jesus then answers the second question, as to His coming. When He comes, this will conclude this present age and usher in the Messianic Kingdom Age [Matthew 24:23].

First, He warns, though people anticipate the Messiah, more pseudo-messiahs will arise, even performing miraculous signs. He says His coming will be as atypical in timing as that rarity, a storm arising out of the East [Matthew 24:24-28]. Generally, a severe storm will arise from the West. Jesus' return, however, will not be so predictable as that. He further implies that as vultures ("eagles") gather to dispose of carrion, false teachers will abound, seeking benefit from a gullible people.

Now, He says, the Messiah will finally come [Matthew 24:29-31]. The conditions prophesied by Joel will come to pass [Joel 2:30-31] and Messiah will come on the clouds with power and great glory. He will come to earth in Jerusalem [Zechariah 14:3-4]. His angels will gather the living elect, in preparation for judgment [Ezekiel 20:33-38] and for entry into the new Kingdom.

Jesus then follows this discourse with further reminders for the people of that time. He says that all those things will occur within the lifespan of the generation living at the time of the end [Matthew 24:34]. No one will be able to precisely pinpoint when that Day will occur [Matthew 24:36].

To cement this idea, Jesus uses an illustration from Noah's day; one that has caused much confusion among Christians over the centuries [Matthew 24:37-41].

He likens conditions at the time of His coming to those of Noah's Day. Despite the fact that Noah had been building his ark for perhaps most of 120 years (the time when God said judgment would come) [Genesis 6:3]. No one took all this seriously, except for Noah. At the time of the Deluge, man was living normally, with marriages and feasts, right up to the time the rains came.

They did not know their judgment had arrived until they were swept away. Only Noah and his family were left, in the ark.

Jesus underscores the seriousness of the coming judgment by comparing it with that earlier event. One was "taken away", another left, He says, using two illustrations. The parallelism should be obvious—those taken away were like those taken away in the flood. Those left are like those left (in the ark). The Greek terms used in Matthew support that idea.

Some Christians insist that those "taken away" refers to the Rapture, but this is directly contrary to the parallelism that the Lord intends.

Jesus concludes with four parables, designed to emphasize the need to be alert and to be doing what one should do, while waiting. The first parable says to "be alert, behave, and beware" [Matthew 24:45-51].

The second parable reminds believers of that day to be equipped to meet the bridegroom and to be expecting to see Him [Matthew 25:1-13].

The third parable warns them to be faithful and fruitful [Matthew 25:14-30].

The final parable deals with the question of what will happen to living Gentiles at the end of this age and how they will be judged. He indicates it will be based on how they assisted living Jews fleeing from the clutches of the Great Man [Matthew 25:31-46].

CHAPTER 16

"Can't Tell the Players without a Scorecard"

In order to fully understand the Great Tribulation, we need to know something about the key players in the scenario. In this chapter, we will consider the First Beast and the Second Beast, who, with the Devil, form an unholy "trinity".

The "First Beast" is seen in [Revelation 13:1-9]. A depiction of the "Second Beast" follows immediately [Revelation 13:10-18]. The unholy trinity is an assumption borne out by the narrative in Revelation [Revelation 13:2]. It is the "dragon" or Devil, who gives power to the First Beast.

The First Beast comes up out of the sea. Many commentators believe this indicates that he will be of gentile origin, for Israel is never associated with the "sea". For almost all of her history, much of the seashore has been controlled by the Philistines or by Rome.

The depiction of this beast as having seven heads and ten crowned horns, links him with the person described by Daniel as the "little horn" [Daniel 7:8], who was one of the leaders of a 10-nation confederacy, and who was to become the predominant personage in that empire. Further information about him is given [Daniel 7:20], which also links him with our First Beast.

The "little horn" of Daniel, chapter eight, is not the same person, but that chapter provides an amazingly precise depiction of the reign of Antiochus Epiphanes IV, who ruled in the middle of the second century B.C. (ca. 165 B.C.). This person (of Daniel eight) is a prototype of the "little horn" of chapter seven.

Chapter nine of Daniel refers again to the "little horn" (of Chapter seven) as the "prince who is to come" [Daniel 9:26]. This provides more insight and corroboration of the activities of this person, placing him directly in the Tribulation period.

Finally, we see him again in the last part of Daniel eleven, which describes his actions during the end of the first half of the seven-year tribulation period [Daniel 11:40-45]. Taken together with the other passages of Daniel, we can see a clear picture of his prominence in the final days.

Another description of this person is found in 2 Thessalonians, where he is described as the "man of sin" [2 Thessalonians 2:3-12]. These passages, viewed together, provide a portrait of a very powerful world ruler, whose rule culminates in the world worshipping him, as described in Revelation thirteen.

This "beast", along with his religious advocate (the "Second Beast") will have the "honor" of being the first human beings to inhabit "Hell" (the "lake of fire", Gehenna; not "Hades"). Hades is the temporary holding place of the souls and spirits of the unsaved dead. This final consignment of the two beasts is spelled out in [Revelation 19:19-21].

We will examine all this in more detail when we get further into the Tribulation period. In this book, I have called this First Beast by the terms: "The Great Man" or "The Great One". In Scripture, he is also called "the man of sin".

The Second Beast is not seen anywhere but in the book of Revelation. He is said to originate from the earth, suggesting that he may be an Israelite [Revelation 13:11-18]. His function is to point people to worship the First Beast. As such, he is probably the head of Religious Babylon [Revelation 17].

Together, as mentioned above, these two form two parts of an unholy trinity, mimicking the Triune God. They receive their power and authority from the Dragon (the Devil) [Revelation 13:2-4; 13:11, 15]. As such, we have the "unholy trinity", with the Devil aping God the Father, the First Beast imitating the Son, and the Second Beast carrying out duties similar to those of the Holy Spirit.

CHAPTER 17

"Can't We All Just Get Along?"

The stage is now set for the time of the "Great Tribulation". There will be a time of relative peace and prosperity, as the Great Man cements his authority over the western world. His religious supporter, the Second Beast steadily mounts a campaign to unite all religions under one banner. He points to the Great Man as worthy of religious adulation (ultimately to morph into worship of him as a god).

One of the insoluble problems facing any world leader for the past 60 years is the issue of the Jewish people in the land they call Israel and which the Palestinians call Palestine. The Jews hold historic Biblical claim to the land as that originally given to them by God.

On the other hand, the Palestinians (mostly Arabs) lay claim to the land through occupation (by some) for 1000 years or more. It is significant to note that the current "Palestinian" people are not descendants of the original Canaanites or Philistines, but are an Arabic people coming from the area now known as Jordan, or beyond.

A seriously-complicating factor is that of the Muslim issue. About 90 per cent of the Palestinians are Muslim. Less than 10 per cent are Christian Arabs, and that number has been shrinking steadily as the Muslims persistently push them out. The Muslims claim Jerusalem as a holy site, for it was from there, supposedly, that Mohammed took his night flight (on horseback) to Paradise for an interview with Allah.

Indeed, the very rock from which he launched his flight is within the mosque known as the "Dome of the Rock". (I actually got to see that rock within the mosque back in 1978.) One may actually see the horse's hoofprints on that rock, some say. (I suppose that may be a "reasonable" notion, for that horse would have had to have a mighty launch, one would imagine).

Additionally, Muslim teaching has it that it was actually Ishmael, not Isaac, who was involved in the sacrificial episode of the Bible [Genesis 22:1-14]. The Jews altered this passage later to fit their own purposes, according to the Muslims. The Arabic Muslims trace their lineage back to Ishmael. And, they say it was Ishmael who was to receive the promises and blessings, not Isaac. Small wonder this is an insoluble problem!

The Temple Mount Area is sacred both to Jew and Gentile. Following the Roman destruction in A.D. 70, except for a brief moment in 1967, the Jews have never been able to use the Temple Mount Area for religious purposes. Indeed, the Dome of the Rock is sited about where the Jewish Temple had been. In order to establish a new Temple, it would be necessary to demolish the Dome of the Rock mosque, built in the seventh century, A.D. In 1967, after capturing the Temple Mount, Israel reached an accommodation with the Arabs that it would not approach the Temple Mount, even though their soldiers would control it.

However, this Great Man is not called the "Great Man" for nothing. Somehow, he will find a way to allow the Jews to sacrifice on the Temple mount (perhaps in the Northeast Corner), without destroying the two mosques currently located on the Mount. It is clear from Daniel that the Jews will be sacrificing sometime during the seven-year period. But that does not necessitate a Temple being built during that time. For example, in the days recorded in Ezra, the people were sacrificing while the foundation of the planned Temple had not yet been laid [Ezra 3:6].

We have no clue as to how the Great Man will be able to pull this off, but it includes a seven-year treaty with Israel, and logically must include an understanding with the Arabs. Such a political coup would resonate strongly with the Jews, and they would naturally give high respect to such a man.

So, the early part of this seven-year period will be one of relative peace and prosperity for the Middle East; an amazing thing in itself. True, the first five Seal Judgments will occur in that period, but these are not part of the "Wrath of God" [Revelation 6:17]. These are natural (though major) consequences God permits as man decides to cast off the God of the Bible. Israel and the Arabs will have some sort of peace accommodation, under the auspices of the Great Man, that also guarantees Israel's security.

In a parallel line, the Second Beast will be drumming up support for establishing a new world religious system, perhaps built along the lines of the old Roman Catholic Church. This is described in [Revelation 17]. We may have a germinal form (at least) in the World Council of Churches and the National Council of Churches. But, it seems likely that both Jew and Muslim (and, probably, Bahai and others) will become part of this new religion, now that the rascally Bible-believing Christians have exited the world scene.

This system will be very powerful and influential and will promote the Great Man's exaltation to deity. However, according to **[Revelation 18:1-8]**, these religionists will be "thrown under the bus", once the Great Man has his deity solidified.

Finally, Chapter eighteen of Revelation suggests a period of unprecedented economic prosperity for the whole world This will be attributed to the power and brilliance of the Great Man. Despite the problems seen in the first five Seal Judgments, it will be a time of great economic promise—but it will come to a crashing end as the Wrath of God begins to fall heavily on mankind.

It is time, now, to examine the second half of the Tribulation, with a brief look at the first five Seal Judgments, followed by the Invasion of Israel which will precipitate the **Day of the Lord** and the balance of the Judgments of God's wrath. But, first . . . .

CHAPTER 18

Babylon, Rome, or Jerusalem?

One of the difficulties in understanding the End Times is in understanding Revelation seventeen and eighteen and the two "Babylons". What are these Babylons? Is there just one, with a religious and an economic flavor? Is this the Babylon in Iraq? Is this a euphemism for Rome? Or, is this a representation of Jerusalem?

If you read different books on the End Times, you will probably find one of these three views:

1) The historic, real Babylon is in view, and the AntiChrist will build his temple there.
2) This is a prophetic look at Roman Catholicism, which would develop in the 4th century A.D., and has been often despised by the Reformers and much of Protestantism.
3) This is a euphemistic depiction of the historic, real Jerusalem in the End Times.

Let's examine the text of Revelation seventeen and eighteen and decide which is the more accurate scenario.

Revelation seventeen describes a religious center in the End Times. It is not a pretty picture of this Babylon. She is called "the great harlot" and is prostituting herself to the political powers of the world. She is riding the First Beast (verse 3). She is rich and ostentatious. She is not part of God's kingdom, but is the antithesis of godly religion. She is in concert with the Great Man and his kingdom, but will finally be stripped of her influence and power.

Revelation eighteen describes a prosperous, economically-thriving metropolis, admired and appreciated by all the world. Yet, in a short, terrible moment, she will crash with incredible speed and be mourned by the world, as she disintegrates.

Okay; is this a reconstructed Babylon? That powerful city, which has remained in desolation for many centuries, under the judgment of God, [Jeremiah 50 and 51], is cursed by God [Jeremiah 51:43]. For many centuries, Babylon has been non-existent, a wasteland. Saddam Hussein of Iraq was attempting to reconstruct the city, with an eye to transferring his capital there. But he did not succeed.

Some competent Bible authorities on the End Times believe that the Great Man will quickly rebuild Babylon and will move his capital there, so as to fulfill the supposed prophecy concernng Babylon in these chapters.While I respect their skill, frankly, I think this is both unnecessary and lacks credibility.

When could this be done? How could this be done, with all the destruction and devastation of the Tribulation period? Why would the Great Man want to remove himself from the center of the three great religions (Christianity, Judaism and Islam) to relocate in a remote area, beginning "from scratch"? That he might wish to contemplate restoring Babylon is entirely possible. But that he could do so within the framework of the seven-year period boggles the mind.

Well, then, could this Babylon be a depiction of Rome, the Roman empire, and the Roman church? There is much to lend credence to this view, with the imagery employed in chapter seventeen. Indeed, following the Reformation, right up into the late 20th century, many waxed eloquent on this seeming parallelism.

There is the city of seven mountains or hills. Rome is famous for being a city of seven hills (Jerusalem also has seven hills). There is the history of collusion by the Roman church with the reigning powers of the Caesars and the "Holy Roman Empire." The depiction of the woman as arrayed in purple and scarlet, with much wealth and pomp and ceremony certainly comes closer to the pomp and circumstance of the Roman Catholic church than perhaps any other religious entity.

The seven kings spoken of in verses 9-11 can logically be identified with seven great kingdoms of the era: Egypt, Assyria, Babylon, Persia, Greece and Rome, followed by the "New Rome" of the End Times.

This is not a very attractive picture of the Roman church, and its validity depends largely on one's view of that church. Frankly, much of the imagery does fit the church, historically. Still, I think that generates an unnecessary and perhaps unfair picture, and, more importantly, masks the idea of a one-world religious entity that I believe is in view here.

The important thing to note is that there will be a world-wide religious power in the time of the Great Man. This will be developed by the Second Beast. He will promote this Great Man as god-like and worthy of worship.

Will it include the Roman church? Probably, along with many Protestant churches. The point is not to single out a particular "Christian" group, for there is much apostasy and heresy in all, particularly at that time. It is that all churches will ally with other religious entities to form this universal religious organization which will have great wealth and influence and be intimately associated with the career of the Great Man.

Indeed, probably every church of whatever "brand" will likely have some members remaining after the cleansing work of the Rapture. Some may be left with just a few. Others may have lost just a handful. But, those who remain will become enamored of the Great Man.

So, that leaves us with the idea that this Babylon is really a euphemism for Jerusalem, which will clearly become the center and capital of the Great Man's empire. This is the simple, logical conclusion, using "Occam's Razor", the idea that the simplest solution is usually the best.one.

Otherwise, we must posit the Great Man coming to Jerusalem, setting up worship, and then transferrring everything to the new Babylon (which must "magically" and quickly arise). We have absolutely no biblical support for such an idea, apart from the name of Babylon itself. That is very thin gruel indeed.

CHAPTER 19

"Tough Times Ahead?"

W e have already suggested that this will be a good time for Israel in the land, as they are promised security by the Great Man himself. He has become the foremost leader in the Western world, and has tremendous political and military influence. All the West looks to him for guidance and support.

However, this IS the world, after all. So, troubles still plague society, in spite of the irenic conditions of peace in the Middle East. The Rapture has occurred. The true church has disappeared. Now man is free to live as he pleases without the nagging presence of Bible-believing Christians. The influence of the Holy Spirit is now thoroughly quenched, as His instrumentality on earth—the true church—is no more. The scene is now set for the opening of the seven Seal Judgments.

While it is true that these Seal Judgments are from God, and are released by the Lord Jesus, the Christ, they are not, strictly speaking, part of the program of the Wrath of God. Rather, they are the natural, logical outcome of the workings of man, now without the restraining influence of the Holy Spirit.

They take the form of 1) political power; 2) various local wars; 3) economic woes generating shortages and hunger; 4) widespread death spread over the globe, as a result of the first three judgments. Man has always had these problems, but now, the impact and scope are intensified. These take place in the first three and one-half years, and are described in Revelation six.

These first four judgments are represented by four horses, (hence, the term "Four horsemen of the Apocalypse").

The first horse illustrates a powerful personage who conquers and gains power without the necessity of war; merely the threat of the possibility of it.

He has a bow, but no arrow is fitted to it. This suggests that no war is needed; threats will suffice. That he is victorious is indicated by the term "conquering", and by the reception of a crown. The horseman represents the Great Man [Revelation 6:1-2].

The second horse is fiery red, and suggests that war will later break out, even though this man comes to power without the use of war. Again, the horseman would likely be the Great Man, who now uses his power to extend his authority by means of conquest, and to foster civil strife within kingdoms [Revelation 6:3-4].

The third horse brings in the inevitable aftermath of war—inflation and shortages. Here again, the horseman is the Great Man, who alone has control of the moneys and foodstuffs of the world. The result is so severe that it is almost impossible for most to do anything more than just survive [Revelation 6:5-6].

This is seen by the materials and prices described. The ordinary working man in the days of John received a denarius for a full day's work. His family would normally consume about a quart of wheat for one meal, barely enough to survive. Therefore, he has to work a full day just to put a minimum amount of food (one meal) on the table. He is living on the sharp edge of poverty, as he has no means to buy clothing or shelter.

Or, he might seek to feed his family with barley products, which are cheaper, but less nourishing than wheat. For his days wage, he can buy three quarts of barley, enough for three meals. He is still in very meager circumstances. The statement about wine and oil indicates that these normal staples of the dinner table are out of the question, as their cost is astronomical.The poor man has no money left over for such things. Thus, once-normal supplements to a meal are unattainable.

The fourth horse depicts the logical and ultimate outcome of such a condition of society. Almost 25 percent of the world's population will not survive these wars, famine, and economic hardships [Revelation 6:7-8].

But, you may say, I thought Israel was living in peace? Well, remember, the Great Man guaranteed them safety and peace, and he also holds the scales of "control" (remember the third horseman), so perhaps he eases up a bit for the Israelis during this time. Besides, living in peace does not necessarily equate to plenty. All the more reason to exalt him, and think of him as Messiah. Further, it is likely that these things occur near the end of the first three and one-half years.

The fifth seal represents the culmination of these events, and describes the Tribulation saints of God (not the church, which is now in heaven), who die or are slaughtered during this period. They are crying out for relief from God. This reminds us that during the entire seven-year period, many will come to a saving knowledge of the Lord. Many of these will become martyrs for their new faith [Revelation 6:9-11].

How does it happen that many are converted to Christ in this time? We'll consider this as we look at the two Witnesses and the 144,000 a bit later. It does remind us, however, of the solemn statements of Jesus as described in [Matthew 24:6-13].

The sixth seal is represented by a huge earthquake, of unprecedented magnitude. Now, finally, the hour of the great **Day of the Lord,** the outpouring of the Wrath of God, has arrived. It is a frightening event. Mankind recognizes this as indeed the Wrath of God. They hide themselves in caves, shaking fearfully at this evidence of God's judgments [Revelation 6:12-17].

A related event is the impending invasion of Israel by forces from the North and from Africa. This will bring the Great Man directly to Jerusalem and will result in His crowning as world ruler and setting up his throne in Jerusalem.

CHAPTER 20

A Squeeze Play

One of the most puzzling parts of the End Times picture is the future invasion of Israel described in Ezekiel 38 and 39. In context, this prophesied invasion clearly occurs in the End Times, based on chapters 35-37. But, just when?

Some say this will occur just before the return of Messiah, at the end of the seven-year Tribulation period. Others suggest it may be placed at the beginning of the Tribulation period, thus accounting for the warfare of [Revelation 6:3].

A good case for either view could be supported. However, on balance, it is likely to occur near the end of the first three and one-half years of the seven-year Tribulation period, for a number of reasons:

- This accounts for the rush of the Great Man through Egypt and to Jerusalem, as recorded in [Daniel 11:40-45]. This helps to explain what prompts the entry of this person into the Middle East. It suggests his motivation is to keep his promise of security to Israel, and supports the fact that he will be the unchallenged ruler of the entire West.
- Further, this occurs at a time when Israel is at peace and feels secure ("unwalled villages") [Ezekiel 38:11]. The only place in Biblical accounting where this could be so would seem to be that time when they feel protected by the treaty with the Great Man [Daniel 9:27].
- It is difficult to imagine armies invading Israel near the end of the Great Tribulation, as this area (as well, perhaps, as their own areas) will have been devastated by the events of the Trumpet and Bowl

Judgments. It is true that a great army will invade the land at the end of the Great Tribulation, thus inciting the battle of Armageddon, but this army will come from the East (perhaps China and/or India).

These two great armies, one from the north of Israel, and one from Egypt, Ethiopia, and Libya will simultaneously attack Israel in a great, crushing pincers movement [Ezekiel 38:1-6]. The northern armies will be a combined effort of perhaps Germany, Russia, Turkey, and Iran.

"Gomer" is usually identified with the Germanic peoples. "Tomargah" is considered to be Turkey and Armenia. "Rosh", "Meshech", and "Tubal" are often identified as "Scythians" (from Southern Russia along the Black Sea). Both Charles Feinberg and Dwight Pentecost so identify these groups.

Israel will be in relative peace, feeling secure without the Wall [Ezekiel 38:11]. Removal of the Wall that we see in modern-day Israel would be likely to happen only in the event of some powerful assurance of security for the people. The attacks will be coordinated and come with great surprise, but Israel will be able to repel them and defeat them, through the influence and intervention of God [Ezekiel 38:17-23 and Ezekiel 39:1-20].

This invasion is a direct threat to the authority of the Great Man and is an insult to him. He will marshal an army, will swoop down the Mediterranean, coursing through North Africa (including Libya, Ethiopia, and Egypt), and race up through Gaza to Jerusalem, coming to the support of his Israelite protectorate. He will have little trouble in Africa, for their armies will have been decimated in Israel and will have fled to the north with their similarly-crushed allies. [Daniel 11:36-45].

Finding the task already completed, he begins to realize that there is no one around powerful enough to challenge him, so he sets himself up as supreme ruler in Jerusalem. There he will be held up to be worshipped through the propaganda efforts of the Second Beast.

Of course, the people of Israel are ecstatic over their victory and over the fact that their benefactor was true to his word and came to protect and support them. His army manages to mop up and destroy the remnants of the invading armies still in pockets in the land, thus enhancing his faithfulness and power [Daniel 11:45].

This sets the stage for the coming New World Order, which is the focus of our next chapter.

CHAPTER 21

The New World Order

W hen the Great Man arrives with his army and entourage in Jerusalem, he discovers that the invading armies have fled north and Israel is busy cleaning up the mess from the war. Ecstatic, he realizes that the last significant threat to his supremacy is over. And, the people of Israel are overjoyed to see him and appreciate his coming to them.

After consultation with the False Prophet (the Second Beast), he decides to move quickly and act boldly to cement his position as leader of the "Free World" (i.e., the West). He begins by opening up food banks to those in need as a result of the war.

Of course, some reasonable controls must be put on this largesse, so he institutes a state-of-the-art identification system that consists of a series of numbers, all beginning with the number 666 **[Revelation 13:16-18]**.

This introductory number will assert that this is a bona fide identification authorized by the Great Man himself. However many following digits may be necessary to add later, this beginning series will serve as a preliminary identifier. A unique style is invented to render it virtually impossible to duplicate.

An edict goes out that everyone now needs to register to get their unique number, which may be inserted in a tiny chip just above their eyebrows, perhaps. For the ladies, it may be inserted on the back of their right hand, so as to avoid any detracting appearance to their face (just kidding, ladies) **[Revelation 13:16-17]**. Trusting this person, who has proven so reliable a protector, many from the Jewish community in Israel quickly sign up and are marked.

The process then rapidly spreads to the Palestinian Arabs and Gentiles throughout the near Middle East. The intention is to mark the entire population of the Western World. At this time, it's feasible only to mark people around the Mediterranean Basin.

Enjoying their work and their planning, the Great Man and the False Prophet, over coffee, decide to further cement this New World Order. They plot to encourage the people to engage in formal worship of the Great Man. The False Prophet is confident he can get his universal religious organization to go along, and he promises to get the Jewish religious leadership in line as well.

At this point, everything is going along quite well. The economy is roaring back from the war deprivations. The people are contented and comfortable, and all are united around the central personality of the Great Man. Accolades are commonplace, not only in the churches, mosques, and synagogues of the area, but are rapidly spreading throughout the entire Western Society.

The leaders now turn their attention to prescribing remedies for the after effects of the wars, famines and inflation that have dogged the world for about three years. In spite of those disasters, the economy is moving forward and the Western World is beginning to realize the dream of a One-World community. Religious differences are set aside or buried, and the few dissenters are quickly rounded up and put to hard labor in restoring Israel in the aftermath of war. Life is good! Well, except for . . .

Some of those pesky Jews. Some of them think it is their mission to get people to trust in that discredited religion—Christianity—and to trust in this Jesus, instead of in the Great Man. Old superstitions die hard, it seems. Rumor has it that some 144,000 Jews have declared that they have the true answer for society and that the Great Man's program is wrong. Orders go out to hunt this group down, and to execute or imprison them as quickly as possible.

Then, the Prophet reminds the Great Man of an even more troublesome pair, who seem to have remarkable powers and are encouraging large numbers to turn to Christ. Mulling it over, it seems best not to arrest them at this time, but to harass them at every opportunity, limiting the scope of their appeal. They have been functioning since the early part of the seven-year entente, and have not had widespread appeal to this point. It seems better not to call attention and notoriety to them, for fear of making them martyrs.

Before long, however, it becomes more and more apparent that these two strange prophets and this gaggle of preaching Jews have become more than a minor annoyance. Increasing numbers of Jews are beginning to have second thoughts about the Great Man, and some resent the amalgamation of their religion with the others. Also, the claims of Christ are beginning to be taken seriously by many Jews and Gentiles As a result, a growing, widespread opposition to worship of the Great Man and refusal to register for the identifying sign is developing, particularly among the young.

Finally, they decide to haul in the two witnesses and they are quickly tried and executed. But, astonishingly, they are reported to have been revived and are back in the streets again. The intensified pursuit of the 144,000 is also backfiring as hundreds, then thousands, and then, tens of thousands of young Jews are fleeing the land, seeking shelter in Italy, Spain, England, and other places, where the identification disks have not yet been fully distributed.

The duo become alarmed, and decide to strike a fatal blow to all of these troublemakers. Before they can mobilize forces to do more, the Western World is staggered by a horrific series of disasters—indeed, so horrific that a great many are crying out that the God of Creation is at work, pouring out disaster after disaster. The buzz on the street is that this is in judgment of the two leaders and on those following them.

Suddenly, their secure perch is tottering. Although efforts continue to hunt down the 144,000 and to do something about the "revived" two witnesses, few apparent results ensue. The devastations make it impossible to carry out all His commands effectively.

Enraged, the Great Man tells the Prophet to disband religion altogether and to dismantle the one world church he had so assiduously courted [**Revelation 18:2-9**]. He turns his focus to rescuing the economic institutions, also reeling under these strange disasters. All religious pretensions are cast aside as delusionary, and all eyes are to be focused on the Great Man. Religion is dismissed as merely a sop or opiate that has outlived its usefulness

With this background, we now turn our attention to the strange outpourings developing from the Wrath of God.

CHAPTER 22

The Wrath of God

A fter our long journey through the background, we finally arrive at a recounting of the coming **Day of the Lord,** with the terrible events so vividly described in the Book of the Revelation. These are not pleasing chapters to read. Indeed, they are frightening in nature. reading them without the background we've plowed through would likely (and, often does) produce skewed, inaccurate views of the nature and purposes of God.

Specifically, the "Wrath of God" is displayed in the last two Seal Judgments **[Revelation 6:12-17 and 8:1-5],** and in the "Trumpet Judgments" **[Revelation 8:6-9:21 and 11:15-19]** and the "Bowl or Vial Judgments" **[Revelation 16:1-21].** As noted earlier, the first five "Seal Judgments" precede the display of the Wrath of God **[Revelation 6:17].**

In considering these awesome events, some further perspective is needed. This is the culmination of God's work with man before He institutes the "Kingdom of Heaven" (which is to be on Earth, not in Heaven). Man has been warned about this for centuries. God's gracious provision for men since the coming of Jesus Christ is for man to receive (welcome) the Lord Jesus as God Incarnate and His Cross work as full payment for their sins.

This is easy enough for anyone to understand and do. Unfortunately, man is forever seeking to justify himself on the basis of his own life and works, and to think of his sins in a lesser light than does God. Man continues to insist that he himself is the measure of his life, not God. Thus, he may miss the grace that is provided freely to him in the Person and Work of the Lord Jesus.

Yet, even during this time of the Wrath of God, many will be saved and many will survive physically, through the testimony of the Two Witnesses and that of the 144,000 Jews. Additionally, just a few years earlier, Christians were on the earth and the Gospel witness was still being given. Man is truly without excuse.

The Sixth Seal [Revelation 6:12-17] is opened with a great earthquake, a darkening of the skies, and unusual disruptions in the heavens. Men begin to realize that the terrible judgment so often threatened in Scripture is beginning. They flee to the caves and rocks of the mountains, in an effort to protect themselves. The summary statement of Revelation Six is telling, "For the great day of His wrath has come, and who is able to stand?" [Revelation 6:17].

Chapter Seven is a parenthesis, giving us an explanation of the nature and purpose of the 144,000 sealed Jews,. There are 12,000 from each tribe.

The Tribe of Dan is missing, here, as is often the case in Scripture. Perhaps this is because from the earliest days of the settlement of the land, Dan has been both rebellious and insignificant.

Originally there were twelve tribes. In the distribution of the land, the sons of Levi were to be priests and own no land [Numbers 1:47-53]. The sons of Joseph, Ephraim and Manasseh, were each given a portion of inheritance [Numbers 1:32-35].

This special group of 144,000, who receive the Lord Jesus after the Church has been removed, have a strong and highly successful ministry [Revelation 7:9]. Some think the reference to the "white robes" suggest many, if not all, were martyred in the seven year period. That may be, but I believe this simply points out that these were clothed in the righteousness of Christ—as indeed will be true for all believers of all ages.

The Seventh Seal is described in Chapter Eight [Revelation 8:1-6]. It is remarkable in that it indicates total silence in Heaven for about 30 minutes (in Earth time). Try creating 30 minutes of absolute silence in yourself and all around you. It's impossible, and a bit unnerving! The point here is that the coming judgments of the Wrath of God are so awesome, so frightening, so devastating that they inspire an awe and fear even among the inhabitants of Heaven. As a side note, this also suggests that, though in Heaven, we will be fully aware of activities on Earth during this seven year period.

Actually, the opening of the Seventh Seal brings forth the first of the Seven Trumpet Judgments [Revelation 8:6-7]. The first judgment is filled with hail and fire, a very unusual, even contradictory event. This hail and fire are "mingled with blood" and pelt the earth. The result is that one-third of the trees and grass are burned up.

The Second Trumpet Judgment shows a large "mountain" (perhaps a meteor?) hurled into the sea (the Mediterranean), and one-third of the Sea becomes "blood", with the result that one-third of sea creatures die, and a third of the shipping is destroyed [Revelation 8:8-9].

The Third Trumpet Judgment has a "star" falling from heaven. In addition to one-third of the sea becoming unusable, one-third of the rivers and springs are no longer viable [Revelation 8:10-11].

The Fourth Trumpet Judgment affects the atmosphere. Apparently, the 24-hour day is shortened for a time to 16 hours. Or, it may simply mean that during the normal daylight hours the light of the sun is darkened for a third of those hours. Notice that there is a problem with light in the night, also. Apparently, one could see neither the stars nor the moon. The end result is very scary and worrisome [Revelation 8:12-13].

The Fifth Trumpet Judgment is picked up in Chapter Nine. This describes Satan and his fall from Heaven [Revelation 9:1-12].

To get a fuller picture of Satan, one should read two important Old Testament passages [Isaiah 14:12-15 and Ezekiel 28:12-19].

In the Isaiah passage, we see that Satan, or Lucifer, is an angelic being who rebelled against God, his Creator. He planned to be on a par with, to be like the "Most High". This brought about his downfall, but it would not be fully carried out until the Tribulation time.

In Job, for example [Job 1:6-12; 2:1-6], we see that Satan still had access to God, after his rebellion. In Revelation, we read that even now, Satan comes before God [Revelation 12:10], accusing the "brethren" (including Christians). But, by the time of the Fifth Trumpet Judgment, He is cast out of Heaven [Revelation 12:9].

In Revelation nine, we see that Satan has the key to the Abyss, or "bottomless pit". It is in this pit that God has held some of the fallen angels, and now Satan sets them free to torment mankind. Who are these fallen angels? Not all fallen angels were put into the pit. Some fallen angels are cast out of heaven with Satan at the time of the end. So, who are these demonic beings from the bottomless pit?

I believe they are the fallen angels described in Genesis [Genesis 6:1-4]. They are referred to by Peter in one of his Epistles [2 Peter 2:4] and by Jude [Jude 6]. These were the "sons of God" (a term often applied to angels, in the Bible), who had sexual intercourse with the "daughters of men". The results of this unholy union were "giants", "mighty men", "men of renown" [Genesis 6:4].

These terms don't do them justice: the Hebrew term translated "giants" refers to powerful beings, often thuggish in nature. Literally, it comes from a verb meaning "to fall upon", "to attack". The second term literally means simply "powerful men of war". The third term literally means "men of notoriety", not exactly a compliment. These demonic beings were frightening in appearance and powerful in practice, and added to the disastrous troubles being heaped on the people of the earth at this time.

Personally, I think what this may be describing is a grotesque aggregation of people (perhaps the "Neanderthals?") resulting from these unnatural relationships. The outcome was the banishment of the fallen angels to the pit, reserved for the Day of Judgment. Incidentally, this "pit" is not Hell. It is merely a holding place. We will discuss that further in another chapter.

But, doesn't the Bible say that [people] "neither marry nor are given in marriage, but are like angels of God in heaven" [Matthew 22:30]? Yes, but we need to consider several things here.

1. People won't marry in Heaven, either. But they do so here on Earth.
2. Angels, as spirit beings, often assumed the characteristics of men, and walked, talked, ate and drank. These fallen angels may have assumed the characteristics of a man, or perhaps took over control of a man.
3. This passage speaks of the proper activity of angels in Heaven. It does not say they are physically sexless (though that may be the case).

A popular (but, wrong, in my view) interpretation is that the "Sons of God" were the males from Seth's line and the "Daughters of men" were the daughters from Cain's lineage. But, if this is so, then all of Seth's offspring would be "Sons of God", that is, "godly". All of Cain's daughters would be "ungodly". This is the idea behind such an interpretation. But that makes no sense. That's quite a stretch.

Furthermore, Enoch [Genesis 5:21-24; Jude 14] preached against ungodliness in that era. Would not some of those likely have been descendants of Seth? Why would Seth's descendant, Methuselah, be taken away with the Flood? A careful study will indicate that Methuselah died in or about the year of the Flood.

This interpretation is a simplistic and erroneous one that depends on the notion that the people of Seth were all "godly ones". Seth seems to have been a good man. Yet he was born in the "image of Adam" (the fallen Adam), not in the "image of God" [Genesis 4:3]. That is a distinction worth noting carefully.

With the Sixth Trumpet [Revelation 9:13-21], we see an immense Eastern army unleashed to wreak havoc on the hapless nations of the Mediterranean regions. The end result of their invasion is the deaths of one-third of mankind.

We need to try to set this into context, so we need another brief digression, in order to better understand all this.

Remember that the Great Man had swept into Israel and established himself in an exalted position in Jerusalem. The armies of the North and of Africa had been defeated by Israel and God. This left a power vacuum for him. There is now no power in the region able to confront him.

However, with the advent of all these terrible judgments, it would be an opportune time for the Eastern World to attack. Their invasion will result in the gathering at Megiddo for the battle of Armageddon. This attacking force will be unleashed near the end of the Tribulation period.

These judgments of the "Wrath of God" (two Seal Judgments, seven Trumpet Judgments, and seven Bowl Judgments) will all occur sometime after the midpoint of the seven-year Tribulation period, perhaps mostly in the final year.

The judgments occur in waves, probably concurrently or in a rapidly-developing crescendo. While the Trumpet Judgments are falling, the Bowl judgments are also being unleashed. Notice the similarities of these two sets of judgments. This explains why the Trumpet Judgments flow out of the Seventh Seal Judgment, and, the Bowl Judgments flow out of the Seventh Trumpet Judgment.

The Seventh Trumpet Judgment is described in Chapter 16 of Revelation. But, before that, we have a parenthetical section from Chapter 10 through Chapter 15 to consider. This interpolation helps to clarify and set the picture for the rest of the story. We will look at this interval in our next chapter, before dealing with the Seventh Trumpet Judgment and the Seven Bowl Judgments.

CHAPTER 23

"Meanwhile, back at the Ranch . . ."

H aving worked our way through most of the Judgments, we encounter a strange six-chapter interlude [Revelation 10 to 15] in the Book of the Revelation. What does this mean, and why this "interruption" of the story?

We are now given more background information to help us better understand the unfolding and to fill in some important details.

Chapter Ten is a brief reminder that God is in control, even as events on the Earth seem to be careening out of control. It reminds us that although the current circumstances of the Wrath of God are wreaking havoc on society, the end result will be sweet [Revelation 10:9]. We are also reminded that God is Creator of all things and all things are within His control [Revelation 10:6].

Chapter eleven tells us of the Two Witnesses who testify for three and one-half years, before being executed. This pair is then miraculously restored to life. They are a powerful witness to the power and grace of God during this terrible time. God is never without His witnesses, and He never neglects to seek and save the lost, even in the time of His Severe Judgment.

Tucked in Chapter eleven is the seventh Trumpet Judgment [Revelation 11:15]. This Judgment signifies that the end is in sight. This will culminate in the opening of the Bowl Judgments.

Much has been written as to the identity of the Two Witnesses and when they operate. Some have identified them as Elijah and Moses, since they carry out similar miraculous signs.

For instance, "waters to turn them to blood" [Revelation 11:6]. This reminds us of Moses' turning the waters of the Nile River to blood [Exodus 7:14-25]. Indeed, you might note the many similarities of the plagues on Egypt with the various judgments in Revelation.

Likewise, the power that no rain falls in the day of their prophecy reminds one of Elijah and the extended drought in the days of King Ahab [1 Kings 17:1-7].

However, there problems with this idea. First, Moses died. These Witnesses both were killed. How could Moses physically die twice, when " . . . it is appointed for men to die once, but after this the judgment . . ." [Hebrews 9:27]? Second, Elijah was carried up to Heaven (or, more accurately, Paradise) [2 Kings 2:1-11]. Would God return him to Earth to die physically, having spared him death originally?

Another problem is that, in both cases, it was the direct action of God producing the waters of blood and the drought. Moses and Elijah were essentially bystanders in these events. Indeed, Elijah experienced the effects of the drought, and Moses certainly did not make any headway with either Pharaoh or the people. In other words, neither of these miraculous effects was done by the direct intention or operation of the men.

I think it is better not to imagine these Two Witnesses as Moses and Elijah. It is pointless to speculate on their identity. They do seem to be mentioned in an indirect way in Zechariah [Zechariah. 4:2-14].

How long do they operate? That's easy. Forty-two months, or 1260 days (30 day months). Yes, but when? In which half of the seven year tribulation? I speculate they minister mostly in the second half, for this is the time that the Great Man holds sway in the region. If so, they would be killed near the end of the second half.

Of course, a case could be made that they will minister in the first half and would be killed shortly after the Great Man seizes full power. In the last analysis, it really is not worth arguing over.

Some background information about the Hebrew calendar will be helpful. The Hebrews used a calendar of twelve 30-day months. They periodically added a month to work everything out. This is why the times noted above and below deal with 30 day increments.

Chapter twelve is a very interesting and informative overview of the whole conflict between God and Satan, with Israel being a very important centerpiece. We need to look carefully at this chapter.

It begins with the picture of a woman crying out in labor and pain while giving birth to a male child, This child was to "rule all nations with a rod of iron" [**Revelation 12:5**]. Clearly this woman represents Israel, who gave birth to Messiah after long and difficult times through the centuries. Some insist the woman is the Church, but the Church did not give birth to Christ. Christ gave birth to the Church.

The fiery red dragon is Satan [**Revelation 12:9**]. He is called the "accuser of our brethren", was in the environs of Heaven, and recognized that he had a limited time to seek to overthrow God's authority. We learn that he is now to be cast out of Heaven, along with the rest of his angels. We have discussed this earlier. His casting out does not occur until the Tribulation [**Revelation 12:7-10**], at the conclusion of a bitter spiritual war in Heaven, which has also spilled over into Earth.

All this takes place in the span of a "time and times and half a time" [**Revelation 12:14**], or 1260 days (three and one-half years of 30 day months). Think of this as an algebraic formula: $X + 2X + 1/2X = 3.5\ X$.

We noted this time frame earlier when looking at Daniel nine. A quick review of all the relevant Scriptures will remind us why we know the Great Tribulation is three and one-half years: [**Daniel 7:25; Daniel 12:7; Revelation 11:2; Revelation 12:6, 14; Revelation 13:5**]. When the Scriptures are this detailed and this precise, it's worth paying careful attention.

Chapter thirteen tells us about the two beasts and the false "trinity" (Satan and the two beasts). We might comment further here on the nature of the sign required of all the beast's worshippers and followers: the sign 666. Much speculation has centered on this over the years, all without merit.

One popular idea that has lasted for a long time is that 666 represents Nero, the Emperor in Paul's day. When writing "Caesar Nero" in Hebrew, it looks something like this [כטר נרין]. (I thought you'd find that helpful! Well, maybe not.) The Hebrews used letters as numbers, and, according to authorities, adding the sum of all these characters give you a number of 666! I don't personally put any stock in such ideas, for a number of reasons, but I'll give you just one, which may settle the issue concerning Nero.

By the time John wrote this Book of the Revelation (about A.D. 90-95), Nero was long since dead. The idea that this would then have meaning to those reading John's Revelation is nonsense. As I mentioned earlier, we have no real idea what the significance is, but the people of the Tribulation period will understand the meaning.

Chapter fourteen provides more information on the 144,000, and describes acts of worship in Heaven as the Tribulation period rolls to its climax. Notice that it is the Son of Man (the Lord Jesus) who wields the sickle in this Judgment.

Chapter fifteen gives us a fascinating image of the victory of God as the Tribulation period draws to an awesome close. It is a vivid reminder that God is Omnipotent, Omniscient, and Omnipresent. He will carry out His plan and program without any lapses or mistakes.

Now, we will consider the final series of Judgments, the Bowl (or, Vial) judgments.

CHAPTER 24

"Let's go Bowling"

W e have come to the final series of Judgments—the Bowl Judgments—as recorded in the sixteenth chapter of Revelation. The Trumpet and Bowl Judgments probably occur in a short span of time (less than the three and one-half years of the "Great Tribulation").

The early part of this second half involves the Great Man consolidating his position as Supreme Ruler, and the Prophet (the second Beast) pulling together the various religious elements left in the world into one global religious system. It is during this time that people will line up to receive the mark which enables them to buy and sell.

Suddenly, some time late in the latter three and one-half year period, God's wrath begins to fall heavily on the people. Throughout I have suggested that this judgment may fall most heavily on the Mediterranean Basin area. However, I do not mean that the rest of the world, including the Far East, is immune from the judgments of God, for this is certainly a world-wide Judgment.

Rather, the Judgments fall most heavily on or about Israel and the Near East, as the center of Biblical history. Perhaps the Eastern powers are just seeking to escape the disasters in their own area. They see the weakness of the Great Man as these devastations fall, and seek to take advantage of it.

The Bowl Judgments complete the Wrath of God [Revelation 15:1]. The First Bowl is described in [Revelation 16:1-2] This is in the form of a "foul and loathsome sore" which comes only on those with the mark and who have worshipped the image of the Great Man.

The Second Bowl completes the disaster of the Sea, begun by the second Trumpet Judgment. The Sea is completely uninhabitable now [Revelation 16:3].

The Third Bowl likewise does the final job on the rivers and springs, begun with the third Trumpet. Now men will find it very difficult to find water to drink or water to relieve the sores [Revelation 16:4-7].

The Fourth Bowl adds to the misery of these people with the sores by increasing the heat and power of the sun on the earth, scorching men with fire. You would think that men now would repent in terror, but they don't. Instead, they continue to curse and blaspheme God [Revelation 16:8-9].

This is a reminder that many will never turn in repentance to God or to Christ. Some will hate God to their dying day. In my more than thirty years of ministry I have seen people like that, hating God, even on their deathbeds.

Imagine for a moment how terrible things must be, with the combined force of the Trumpet and Bowl Judgments poured out. Think of the misery of the hot and hurting power of the sun, now magnified on the earth. There seems to be no escape from the burning and the brightness of this terrible time.

The Fifth Bowl introduces misery and torture of an entirely different nature. Men who wore dark glasses and heavy protective clothing to shield themselves from the intense heat and light of the sun, now find themselves suddenly in pitch darkness, poured out on those in the kingdom of the Beast. But, once again, they confirm the justice of their judgment, lashing out at God in their pain and anquish. At no point do they think they should change allegiance. Amazing! [Revelation 16:10-11].

Now, the outpouring of the Sixth Bowl brings a climax to the wickedness generated by the unholy trinity. First, the Euphrates River is dried up (probably from the third Bowl Judgment), making it easier for the million-man Eastern Army to move in on Israel. Then, all the fallen angels (the demonic beings) are fully unleashed, to incite and plague the people, as the Dragon throws in his reserves into this all-out confrontation with God [Revelation 16:12-16].

All these armies gather near Mount Megiddo (Har Megiddo, in the Hebrew language), a small rise just west of the great Valley of Jezreel and Plain of Esdraelon [Hosea 1:5; Joel 3:14]. They are organizing for a great pitched battle between the Great Man's army and the Eastern Army. The end is now near. The great battle of Armageddon is about to begin, urged on by these destructive demonic forces. This is an awesome reminder that the forces of evil are always not only destructive, but are always self-destructive in the end.

I have been to Megiddo twice, and have gazed over this vast open area. It is amazingly large and open and flat; unusual for this tiny land of Israel. Megiddo has been fortified many times by various forces, and has been the scene of countless battles and attacks. But this one is the "mother of them all".

I have no idea how many soldiers could be accommodated at one time in this vast area, but it would surely be a very large number. And, as is always true in battles, a large percentage of the armies are in the rear areas, awaiting combat or providing support and supplies.

Just as the two opposing forces are about to engage in battle, the Seventh Bowl is opened, spewing out an intensely-powerful earthquake [**Revelation 16:17-21**]. Jerusalem is split in two [**Zechariah 14:3-4**]. Huge hailstones (about 100 pounds each) fall, and men continue to blaspheme and curse God.

The Lord Jesus, the Christ, suddenly appears, coming down from Heaven with the armies of Heaven [**Revelation 19:11-21**]. The two opposing armies in the valley of Jezreel then unite to oppose their common enemy, Christ. But they are quickly destroyed by the power of His word. Thus ends the "Battle of Armageddon".

We reviewed chapters seventeen and eighteen of Revelation earlier. We can now move on to trace the commencement and events of the Millennial Kingdom. We will define the inhabitants of that kingdom and their qualifications for entry. We will see the judgment of God on the unholy trinity.

Then, we will take a look at life in that Kingdom, followed by the release of Satan and the final "Armageddon'. We will conclude with a look at the New Heaven and the New Earth.

CHAPTER 25

"Going to Hell?"

W hen the Lord returns to this Earth, He will do so as Conqueror, King of Kings and Lord of Lords. His return is described in Matthew, in Revelation, and in Psalms and Zechariah, among other places [**Matthew 24:27-31,36-44; Revelation 19:11-21; Psalm 2, Psalm 24, and Zechariah 14:3-9**].

He will institute His 1000-year rule over the Earth [**Revelation 20:2-7**]. He will send the two Beasts (the Great Man and the False Prophet) directly to the true Hell (Gehenna, the Lake of Fire) [**Revelation 19:20**], and will thrust Satan into the Abyss, the Bottomless Pit. Satan will be confined there for the entire 1000-year period [**Revelation 20:2-3**].

The very first inhabitants of the Lake of Fire will be the two beasts, consigned there at the end of the Tribulation period. And, with Satan being bound, mankind will have no problems with him throughout the Millennial Reign.

There is confusion among Christians as to "Hell", due largely to inadequate translations, "Hell", is actually "Hades", the place of the souls and spirits of the dead, both saved and unsaved. In fact, "Hades" is ultimately cast into the "Lake of Fire" [**Revelation 20:14**]. Thus, they could not be the same. No Old Testament Saint (Enoch and Elijah likely went to Paradise, which is not Heaven) went to Heaven. They had to wait for their Redeemer to precede them, for He is the "First Fruits".

The believers were housed in "Paradise" or "Abraham's Bosom", a compartment of Hades. The unsaved were housed in the other compartment of Hades, and there was an unbridgeable division between them [**Luke 16:19-31**]. Now, I realize that is a parable, but it sheds insight on a difficult problem.

Why doesn't the Old Testament differentiate between "Hades" and "Paradise"? Because there is no point or purpose to do so, for all the spirits of all the dead are housed in Hades. In this parable, Jesus provides information that helps us to understand several other events. When He told the trusting thief on the cross "Today you will be with Me in Paradise" [Luke 23:43], He meant exactly that. He did not mean "Heaven", for Jesus Himself did not go to Heaven that night.

When Christ ascended triumphantly into Heaven [Acts 1:9-10], He led in his wake the souls and spirits of all the Old Testament saints [Ephesians 4:8]. These could not precede their Savior into Heaven, so they awaited Him in the compartment of Hades called "Paradise".

The "captives" described there are those often referred to in the Old Testament, and almost always are speaking of believers. Our study does not permit me to cover that in detail, but I would challenge you to look up "captives" and "prisoners" in a concordance, and you would see what I mean. Here are just a handful of such references, to get you started: [Obadiah 20; Amos 9:14; Zechariah 9:11-12; Psalm 53:6; Psalm 68:16; and Psalm 69:33].

But, when were the Old Testament saints resurrected, or when will they be? Actually, their bodies will be resurrected at the beginning of the Millennial Age [Daniel 12:1-2]. This will occur after the Great Tribulation. All the believers of the Church age will have been resurrected by that time, as their resurrection or change comes before the Great Tribulation [1 Thessalonians 4:13-17].

Another passage that is often interpreted in a confused manner is that found in 1 Peter [1 Peter 3:18-20]. This passage was used to support the idea long-held that Jesus descended into "Hell"; He did not. He descended into Hades, and more precisely, into the compartment called "Paradise". How can I be so sure?

Since there is no one in "hell" (meaning the final Hell, Gehenna, the Lake of Fire) until the two beasts are sent there at the end of the Tribulation [Revelation 19:20], there would be no point in Jesus going there. There would be nobody to see there. Secondly, the idea that the resurrected Jesus would go into the place where ultimately Satan will "rule" is nonsensical.

Some have said that Jesus descended into Hell in order to preach to the condemned there, thus giving them a second chance. But this is totally contrary to Scripture [e.g., Hebrews 9:27]. Others have said that He descended into Hell to formally condemn the already-condemned. But all this is due to failure to realize that Hades is not "Hell".

It is true that the place of the unsaved dead in Hades is not a pleasant place, but it is still not the final Hell. In fact, no human being (apart from the two Beasts) will go into Hell (Gehenna) until Satan is sent there at the END of the Millennial reign [**Revelation 20:10**].

So, where did Christ go and what did He do there? He descended into Paradise (the "good" compartment of Hades) and announced to the spirits and souls of the Old Testament saints that they would be going with Him soon to Heaven, to await their bodily resurrection at the institution of the Millennial Kingdom.

Now, it's time to see just who will populate the Millennial Kingdom, and by what criteria.

CHAPTER 26

"Passports, Please!"

J ust who will be eligible to live in the Millennial Kingdom? What are the qualifications and criteria? Let's take a look, beginning with some basic factors:

- Not all human beings alive at the end of the Tribulation will go into the Millennial Kingdom.
- Every one who enters the Millennial Kingdom at the end of the Tribulation will be a saved person, saved through the atoning blood of Jesus Christ.
- Living Jews will be judged directly by Christ, before they can enter the Millennial Kingdom [Ezekiel 20:33-38].
- Living Gentiles will be judged based on their treatment of fleeing, believing Jews [Matthew 25:31-46].
- The Old Testament saints (of all eras, including those before the Mosaic Law) will be resurrected and will be involved in the Millennial Kingdom, as guides and leaders [Matthew 8:11; Luke 22:30; Ezekiel 37:11-14].
- The Raptured Church will be with Christ and will assist Him in judging Millennial Kingdom people and activities. They will also be in their Resurrection bodies [Matthew 19:28; 1 Corinthians 6:2; Revelation 3:21].
- David will be the King or Prince of Israel, and will be under the Lord Jesus Christ, who will be King of Kings and Lord of Lords [Isaiah 55:4; Jeremiah 30:9; Ezekiel 34:23; Ezekiel 37:25; Hosea 3:5].

Many of the Jews who have turned to Christ during the Tribulation period, and are still alive at the end of that period, will have fled Israel, as the Great Man demands their worship. They will run as far from his authority as possible.

When Christ comes to Earth, He will call all living Jews from every corner of the globe, both believing and unbelieving, to the Wilderness of Judea. There He will verify which ones belong to Him [Ezekiel 20:33-38].

He will work in a fashion employed by sheepherders. The shepherd calls his sheep to an enclosed sheep cote at dusk. He has a narrow entry—gate, and uses his shepherd's crook (staff) to sort out his sheep from others. If one of his flock seeks to enter the fold, he will lift his staff from across the gate, so the sheep can go in to safety. However, if a strange sheep approaches, the shepherd will bar the gate with his staff to prevent entry. This is the imagery seen in this passage. (Note: the judgment is literal, but the methodology is metaphorical.)

Those living Jews who are not Christ's will not only be denied entry into the land of Israel, but they will be purged, and presumably executed, for only believers will live in Israel and throughout the world, both Jew and Gentile. Numerous Old Testament passages indicate that all who enter the Millennial Kingdom will know the Lord [cf. Isaiah 56:6-8].

Gentiles will be judged according to the mercy shown the fleeing Jews. At great personal risk, they will defy the orders of the Great Man and give whatever shelter they can to the Jews. This is similar to that seen in Europe in the Second World War, when many Gentiles sheltered Jews from the Germans. Even today, in Israel, these Gentiles are honored by the Jews, at the Holocaust Museum in Jerusalem, as the "Righteous Gentiles". That is the idea seen in the judgment on the Gentiles [Matthew 25:31-46].

David will be the local King of Israel, or their Prince. He is the Prince seen in [Ezekiel 44:1-3; 45:7, 16; and 46:1-18]. This "Prince" is often erroneously identified with Christ, but a review of these passages [Isaiah 55:4; Jeremiah 30:9; Ezekiel 34:23; Ezekiel 37:25; Hosea 3:5] will show that this is David, not Christ, for the Prince in [Ezekiel 40-48] owns land in Israel and gives sacrificial offerings, among other things.

The passages noted earlier in this chapter concerning a resurrected David are self-explanatory. David will be the King of Israel; Christ will be King over the entire Millennial Kingdom, including Gentile lands such as Egypt and Syria [cf. Isaiah 19:18-25].

The Church (that company of believers formed on the Day of Pentecost in A.D. 33 and continuing until the Rapture) will be with the Lord Jesus Christ, wherever He is. As He rules on Earth, they will rule with him. They will be in resurrected bodies and may "commute" between Heaven and Earth during this Millennial reign.

What about the believers who come to a saving knowledge of God during the Tribulation? We are given no direct information on that, except that there will be a great number of them. We may presume they will be given Resurrection bodies, probably at the beginning of the Millennial Kingdom. But, it is important to understand that they are not the Church or part of the Church. They are another of the "households of God", along with those described in our chapter on Dispensations.

We will now explore the characteristics of the wonderful Millennial Kingdom (or, the "Kingdom of Heaven", as Matthew describes it).

CHAPTER 27

"Life is Good!"

We've already learned about a number of features of life in the Millennial Kingdom. Among these are:

- The Kingdom will be on Earth.
- It will last 1000 years.
- It will begin with living, believing Jews and Gentiles.
- The Old Testament saints will be resurrected and active among the living believers.
- Israel will be ruled by a resurrected David.
- Satan will be absent, along with demons, for the entire time.
- Jesus, the Christ, will be Absolute Master over the entire Earth, as King of Kings and Lord of Lords.
- The Church will not inhabit the Millennial Kingdom, although they will play a part in judging and guiding.

Now, let's look at other important features of this remarkable time.

- Many will likely live through the entire age, as long life will be the norm [Isaiah 65:20-22].
- Anyone who rebels against Christ will be summarily executed or punished [Isaiah 65:20].
- The Earth will be Eden-like in its quality [Isaiah 32:15; 35:6-8; 41:18-19; 51:3; 55:12-13].

- There will be death during this time, though rare [Isaiah 65:20].
- The animal world will no longer be predatory or subject to predators; all will become vegetarian [Isaiah 65:25].
- The animal world will no longer fear or harm humans [Isaiah 11:6-9].
- There will be a Jewish Temple, and Gentiles from around the world will come to worship in it [Isaiah 60:1-11, 13; 66:18-23; Ezekiel 40:5].
- There will be animal sacrifices in the Jewish Temple [Isaiah 56:6-8; Ezekiel 43:18-27].
- The Rule of Law will not be the Mosaic Law, but rather the laws of the Kingdom. These have been revealed in Biblical teachings about the "Kingdom of Heaven", seen primarily in the Synoptic (Matthew, Mark, Luke) Gospels.
- The Jews will celebrate Passover and the Feast of Tabernacles [Ezekiel 45:18-25].
- There will no longer be a Day of Atonement (Yom Kippur) [Ezekiel 40-48, omitted].
- There will no longer be Pentecost (Feast of Weeks) [Ezekiel 40-48, omitted].
- Life will be pleasant and peaceful [Isaiah 60:21-22; 61:4-7; 65:21-22].
- There will be no wars, graft, robberies, or murders [Isaiah 2:1-4].
- All living believers at the beginning of the Millennial Kingdom will be born again
- The Spirit of God will be poured out on them [Joel 2:28-29; Isaiah 32:15; 44:3; Jeremiah 24:7; 31:33; 32:39; Ezekiel 11:19; 18:31; 36:26; 37:14; 38:29; Zechariah 12:10].
- People will marry and have children during the Millennial Kingdom [Isaiah 49:20; 54:13; 61:9-10; 65:20, 23].
- The hearts and attitudes of people will be similar to the minds and attitudes of true Christians of today. They will still be capable of sin, but the motivations from Satan will be absent. Punishment for disobedience toward God will be swift and severe.

Because there are so many points here, I thought it best to simply provide some supporting Scriptures and to encourage you to look them up. There are many more to be found. Enjoy searching them out.

This Kingdom will be a glorious one—very much like Eden before the Fall. However, those in the Kingdom are living, breathing human beings, with a sin nature. Still, at the beginning of the Kingdom Age, every one entering is a true believer in Jesus, the Christ.

They will have children and grandchildren [Isaiah 65:20-23]. Some of these may not truly trust Christ. They will keep their view quiet, for outward rebellion would result in sure judgment. When Satan is loosed from the Abyss at the end of the thousand years, he will be able to enlist these silent rebels in his new army.

The common notion held in Reformed Theology is that all these prophecies relating to a future Israel are really euphemisms for grace dispensed to the Church. But, in the face of so much clear Scripture, they are forced into a contrived interpretation in order to dismiss the prophetic word about the future Israel. This euphemistic interpretive notion is truly in error and misleading.

This view is based on the idea the Israel has been supplanted by the Church. Thus, future blessings are for the Church. The separation of the Church from Israel (but not the supplanting of Israel) is a crucial doctrine, essential for understanding the prophetic word properly. It is important to have a consistent interpretational approach. We should take all Scripture at face value, unless it is obviously symbolic.

This is also central to a proper understanding of the "Kingdom of Heaven" described in Matthew. That Kingdom is centered on Earth, not in Heaven. Failure to understand this has often led to teaching to place individual Christians under law again—Kingdom law (different, but related to the Law of Moses). This has led to much faulty interpretation and application of the Synoptic Gospels in particular, and to much confusion and even contradiction in Christian teachings.

These passages in Matthew (and supported in Mark and Luke) are intended to mark out Kingdom Law, not a set of laws for Christians today. Kingdom Law is a heightened and tightened derivative of the Mosaic Law. Read [Matthew 5:19-48] to see just how Jesus stresses the internal requirements. The Mosaic Law deals with externals; the Kingdom Law deals with the internals of the heart.

Satan is bound, and Eden-like qualities on earth abound during this Kingdom Age. Also, the fact that all are believers makes a holy life feasible and sensible.

As is true in the Old Testament, we may derive principles of God's thinking from them, but they are not law for the church. An example or two may suffice to show the folly of such misinterpretation:

- **[Matthew 5:5]**, "Blessed are the meek, for they shall inherit the earth".

  o Does this mean that you and I (as Christians) can expect to acquire a parcel of the Earth, during the "Kingdom of Heaven"? Of course not.

- **[Matthew 7:1]**, "Judge not, that you be not judged. For with what judgment you judge, you will be judged."

  o Does this mean that I will be judged and condemned in Heaven for my judging ways? Of course not, for Christ died for my sin and sins, including a sin of being judgmental.

We can draw principles for behavior, but they are not laws for us. In fact, all our sins have been laid on the Lord Jesus Christ. We will be accepted into Heaven purely on the basis of our acceptance and trust in His finished work on the Cross. The condemnatory judgment is finished.

We will now move on to the new heavens and new earth, which are described so well in **[Revelation 21 and 22]**.

CHAPTER 28

Thinning the Ranks

At long last, God's Plan for the Ages is complete. This old Earth, so important for so long, is to be replaced by a wonderful new Earth, blended with a new Heaven. That is really more than we can imagine.

God has shown man by different experiences, throughout human history, that man can never accomplish God's purposes. Nor can he reap the benefits of God's grace by his own efforts, no matter how well-intended.

Man entered this world by Divine fiat—God spoke the world and man into existence [Genesis 1 and 2]. Man entered this world, created especially for him [Genesis 1:28; 2:15-17], in a state of innocence. Man relied totally on his Creator for guidance and direction. He did not contemplate evil, and God provided only good.

Man was given instructions on what to eat. He was free to eat of any and every tree of the Garden of Eden, except the "tree of the knowledge of good and evil" [Genesis 2:16-17]. Man was to rely totally on the direction of God. Remarkably, he had only one negative to deal with in all of Eden.

Satan, already at war with God, entered the Garden in the form of a serpent. He subtly encouraged them to trust his judgment over that of God [Genesis 3:1-7].

They ate of the forbidden fruit and their entire relationships were changed, forever. God did not abandon them, but provided clothing for them, and promised them [Genesis 3:15], that one day a Man would be victor over Satan. Their souls were blackened with the sin of rebellion. Their spirits, with which they once could commune directly with God, were deadened.

This event, which brought a similar condition to all their progeny, is called "The Fall". Their sin was not in committing some heinous deed such as murder or adultery, but in trusting the word of the serpent, rather than to trust the word of God.

Man still does that today, even if his behavior is "good". He either disobeys the commands of God or he simply ignores God. Either way, this is an illogical, senseless and devastating sin. He refuses to live with God or he shuns God. Small wonder, then, that he lives a life of pointlessness and uselessness.

Now man could imagine all sorts of evil, and would also develop ideas of "good" according to his own opinions. The problem is that, adrift from the direction of his Creator, man always mars even his "good" works. Man has suffered ever since, and the consequence was evil of such a gross nature that God destroyed man in the Great Flood [Genesis 6-8].

After the Flood, God launched mankind into a new era, where one family, headed by a patriarch, would populate a new society. As we saw earlier, God provided some additional instructions on how to live, and He changed the environment. Perhaps, man might think, now, with everybody related and with more rules and guidelines, man would surely be good. But, they weren't, as the Tower of Babel episode [Genesis 11:1-9] showed. Man developed false gods as idols. Men engaged in wars and slavery and increased in immoral behavior.

Then, God re-directed mankind, or rather, a small segment of mankind, by dealing specially with Abram, providing him new directions, beyond those previously given. God gave Abram direction and information on how to approach and serve God. God guided him to a new locale, which God promised would belong one day to Abram's progeny.

From this special beginning with Abram, God narrowed the field further, through Isaac and Jacob, down to Jacob's sons. In doing this, God was again re-establishing the closeness and primacy of family relationships, hearkening back to the days of Noah. God cared for this small tribe for centuries, allowing them to lapse into servitude to the Egyptians, finally rescuing them through Moses.

God now provided this small band of Hebrews (by the time of the Exodus, perhaps as many as one or two million) a new land that would be fruitful. He brought victory over the peoples of the land and of the surrounding area. God provided them with a very detailed and specific "constitution", the "Mosaic Law", or Law of Moses, that was to guide them in all areas of life: Religious, Political, Economic, Personal and Social.

However, once again, man failed to maintain a proper relationship with his Creator, plunging into various sins, idolatry, arrogance, and intrigues (see

Joshua and Judges). After some 400 years, God granted the Israelites' request for an authoritative and controlling King. The people thought they would then live like their neighbors (and, they did, but tragically). Of course, that failed, with the eventual loss of the kingdom entirely, after more than 400 years, with the Babylonian Captivity.

Then, God did an utterly new work, carving out a new "tribe" related not by the blood sacrifices of their forefathers, but by the blood shed by God's own Son, the Lord Jesus, the Christ. The old divisions of Jew and Gentile were erased. Both could become a part of this entirely new entity.

We have now lived some 2000 years in this situation, and it clearly is not the answer, as man continues to slide into debauchery and denial of God. And this slide will develop at breakneck speed once the church is removed at the Rapture. Then, man has to experience the judgment of God in the Great Tribulation.

Satan will be bound for 1000 years. The Earth will become Eden-like, once again. All who enter the new society are believers in God and Christ, and things are good.

But, once Satan is loosed from the Abyss, he is able to gain the allegiance of some of the children and grandchildren in a short-lived rebellion **[Revelation 20:7-10]**. This will be followed by the Great White Throne Judgment **[Revelation 20:11-15]**.

This Great White Throne Judgment is the final judgment of all of the unbelieving (unsaved) of every age, dating back to the very beginning. Contrary to popular opinion and interpretation, no human being (apart from the two "beasts") enters the final Hell: the Lake of Fire or Gehenna until the Great White Throne Judgment is completed.

Interestingly, men are not judged for their sins, but for their "works". I believe Christ is saying to them, "So, you wish to be evaluated on your own merits? Fine; trot them out, and let's examine them." A picture of this is seen in Matthew **[Matthew 7:21-23]**.

Why are they not judged for their sinful deeds? Because the Lord Jesus has paid the penalty for all the sins of all mankind. Why doesn't this help them at this time of judgment at the Great White Throne **[Revelation 20:11-15]**? Because they prefer to be evaluated on their own merits, rather than on the merits of Christ. Whatsoever is not of faith is sin, so even the works which they deem to be valid and praiseworthy fall short, because Jesus never "knew them". They lacked a personal relationship with God, trusting in themselves rather than in God's gracious provision in Christ.

No one will pass this final judgment. All will be consigned permanently to Gehenna, there to join Satan **[Revelation 20:10]** and the two beasts forever. What is this final Hell really like? It is an eternity of existence totally separated from God. Think of it: God is Good. God is Truth. God is Pure. God is Holy. Now, realize that the absence of God guarantees an absence of Good, Truth, Purity, and Holiness, among other things—forever!

Think of the absolute worst conditions or activities that man has ever devised through the ages—then, multiply that by some immense factor. That's how bad it will be.

With this, we are ready now to experience the ultimate—the New Heaven and New Earth.

CHAPTER 29

"Finally! We've Arrived!"

The last two chapters of the Book of the Revelation provide interesting insights into our final destination. This will be the final destiny of all those, through all the ages, who have believed God and had it accounted to them for righteousness. Following the 1000-year millennial reign of Christ, an entirely new creation will unfold. There will be a new heaven and a new earth, where all God's people of every age and every era will be gathered together.

The saints in heaven will come to the new earth. The Church will come to the new earth. The people of Israel and the Old Testament saints will come to the new earth. The Tribulation and the Millennial saints wll come to the new earth. Those distinctions will cease to exist. All will be God's elect.

The heavenly city, the new Jerusalem, will come down from heaven and be located on the new earth. God Himself, with His Son, and with His Holy Spirit, will also "vacate" heaven and be "located" in the new earth. There will be no more tears, no more death, no more sorrow, no more crying, and no further pain.

This is to be the final abode of God and all His people. None who rejected Him, whose characters are entirely incompatible with that of God, will be there. Rather, they will abide forever in the Lake of Fire, experiencing the "second death" [Revelation 20:14].

This new Jerusalem will have a great, high wall, and will be a true city of light, brighter than the brightest gems. There will be twelve gates, with the names of the twelve tribes inscribed; three on each side of the city. There will also be twelve foundations with the inscribed names of the twelve apostles.

The city is immense; quite unlike anything ever seen or imagined. It will be some 1400 miles on each side, and will extend into the heights to 1400 miles! The beauty of the city is beyond imagination. The "emerald city" of Oz, in the movie, "The Wizard of Oz", is perhaps as close as we can come in our imaginations.

There will be no need of a light source, not even that of the sun or moon. For the Shekinah Glory of God will be sufficient to keep every nook and cranny well-lighted. The gates will never be closed, for there is no need of protection.

Within this wonderful city, there is a flowing river, proceding from the throne of God and the Lamb. It will be constantly fruitful and will provide constant "healing" for all. The curse on the land is gone. Devotional service toward God and His Lamb will be a joy and delight.

Unlike the branding of the followers of the false messiah of Revelation, all the people will have the name of the Lord Jesus on their foreheads, as a testimony to His grace. This marvellous condition shall have no end. All the inhabitants will be recorded in the Book of Life. The Tree of Life shall be in the center of this marvellous city. There will be peace, joy, fellowship with people of all eras and ages, and eternal bliss.

At this point, let's take a moment to consider the way one truly becomes a Christian. It is not by joining a church, not by being baptized, not by walking an aisle or saying a prayer, not by association with Christians, and not by "knowing" the Bible.

Salvation is full, free and final, and is received by:

- *Recognizing* my inadequacy and my sin. Man's fundamental sin is in ignoring or opposing our Creator. All our sins flow out of that absurdity. Even our best works, when placed against the perfection that is Heaven and the perfection that is God the Creator, fall far short. No matter how good I seek to be and no matter how long I might live, I will never measure up to the standard of perfection with God. In fact, I will never even keep my own standards perfectly [**Romans 3:10-20**].
- *Recognizing* that I will always fall short, perfection can be credited or provided to me only by one who is perfect. And that credit can only be valid if my discredits (sins) are fully dealt with [**Romans 4:16-25**].
- *Accepting* the full payment for my sin and sins in the finished work of God's Son, the Lord, Jesus, the Christ. He died in full payment as an atoning sacrifice for my sin and my sins. Since He is perfect, His work

is sufficient to erase my sins, no matter their number or magnitude [2 Corinthians 5:18-21].

- *Turning* to the Lord Jesus, asking Him to be my Savior, trusting only and always in His work as complete and sufficient satisfaction for my salvation [John 1:12].

If you have not done that; if you are trusting in your own works or those of some other person or group for acceptance with your Creator, stop! Change your mind (repent) about your sin and your works. Cast yourself on the mercy of God. Turn to the Lord Jesus now. He will save you—immediately, and for ever!

This is so simple that anyone can avail himself of it, whether young or old, rich or poor, "respectable" or despicable, intelligent or illiterate, male or female. healthy or infirm—anyone.

Find a Bible-believing, Bible-teaching person or church and become discipled in the written Word of God, the Bible. Grow in grace as you learn more of the wonderful heritage that is now yours.

CHAPTER 30

From Here to Eternity?

We have considered God's plan for mankind and this old earth in some detail. We have begun at the beginning. We have traced His hand and plan through all the various eras and ages. We have seen that His Word and His program blend together into a beautiful mosaic. We've seen the bright beauty of His grace, manifested in many different ways. We also see the stark, harsh colors of His judgment; He is not mocked.

And so, here we are today, somewhere in the lifeline of His plan. What do we do? Where do we head? What should we plan? How shall we live? Where are we on the spectrum of His work?

We realize that we are now closer to the end than ever before. We know that the Rapture has not yet come. Nor has the Great Tribulation arrived. We see all around us evidences of increasing disarray and decay. We observe that man's activities are clearly as horrific as described in Romans [**Romans 1:18-32**].

We shudder at the thought that things will continue to get worse and worse, as Paul warned Timothy [**2 Timothy 3:1-7**]. We are disheartened to realize that even who claim the name of Christ will rush down the primrose path of disobedience and destruction at an ever-increasing rate [**2 Timothy 4:2-4**]. True, there may be seasons of improvement and relief, but we're warned that these will become fewer and farther between.

What can we do? Are we helpless against this rising crescendo of hating God and all He has revealed? Attacks on the Bible and on genuine Christians is increasing exponentially. Good is being called evil. Evil is being called good. Increasingly, Bible-believing Christians are said to be fanatics and enemies of society. Are we doomed to simply be swept along with the tide? Should we rejoice at the rapidly-increasing lawlessness and self-interest, knowing that the end is near?

We need to realize, first of all, that we are in the midst of a spiritual warfare, a worldwide rebellion against the God of the Bible. This is not a new thing, but traces back to before Adam and Eve, when Lucifer first rebelled against God [Isaiah 14:12-15; Ezekiel 28:12-15]. Man was enlisted in this war by the serpent in the Garden of Eden. Eve and Adam chose to follow the advice of an unknown against the specific commands of a gracious God.

As history has unfolded, man persistently chooses any and every counsel except that of God. The results are always devastating to man. The psalmist reminds of this ongoing warfare [Psalm 2:1-3]. The accounts of countless men and nations recorded in Scripture provide constant reminders of foolish attempts by man to be his own master. Seldom has he realized that his true master is Satan [Ephesians 2:1-3].

Yet, also throughout Scripture we see the hand of a gracious, loving, forgiving God. He is indescribably patient with our sins and foibles. His love and grace have been manifested in an amazing fashion. He sent His Son, the Lord Jesus, to be our sin-bearer. God laid all the sins of the world on Him at Calvary. Jesus became the true Scapegoat, as well as the true Sacrificial Lamb [Hebrews 9:12-14; 9:26-28; 10:10-12].

God did all this that He might impute (reckon) every one of our sins and our sin on Christ [Romans 4:1-25]. He imputes sufficient of His Son's inexhaustible purity to our account, enabling us to stand clothed in the righteousness of Christ [Romans 4-6]. What we could never do for ourselves, trapped as we are in our sin nature, God has graciously done for us. And the cost to us? Only our pride! We must come to the cross naked, without any attempt at claiming merit, where we will be graciously received.

This spiritual warfare was evident not only in Biblical times, but continued on through the centuries. We see the barbarity of Rome, the excesses of Islam, the rise and fall of powers through the centuries. We see the continuing attempts to stamp out the Jews: the pogroms, the persecutions, the Holocaust, the attempts to crush tiny Israel.

We see a concerted effort in our own nation in the 1960's to crush all evidences of a Judeo-Christian morality and ethos, to be replaced by an existentialist, anarchist "nirvana". Today, we are still reaping the bitter fruits of that effort. The details are different. The methodology has shifted. The goal is the same.

The desire is to dismantle America as we knew it, and replace it with their "brave new world", making indelible changes in virtually every aspect of life. And, certainly, there are justifiable criticisms of this Judeo-Christian mindset. But, with all its failings, it is grounded to some degree on the God of the Bible. This must go, say our modern reconstructionists.

What can we do? The answer is the same as it has been through every age. Trust God's Revelation, the Bible. Fortify yourself with the Word of God [2 Timothy 2:15]. Know your enemy (Satan) and his ploys [Ephesians 4:14; 2 Corinthians 11:13-15]. Seek the counsel and wisdom and comfort that only God can provide.

Sadly, we Christians today are too often virtually illiterate in the Word of God. True, we may know some of the Bible stories learned in childhood: Noah and the Ark, Daniel in the Lion's den, Jonah and the great fish, among others. Yet, far too frequently, we have only a feeble grasp of the whole Bible. We need a cohesive, coherent understanding of all of God's Revelation.

And then we are at risk of victimization by any wind of doctrine or by those who teach deceiving words and ways, turning the Word of God into syrupy modernistic "feel-good" stories.

This is why I've chosen to write about the End Times in this fashion, covering so much of the entire Bible. I want us all to see the progression and interlacing of His Word. This is why I've included so many Scripture references and entered them in a manner to call attention to them. It is my hope that, having read this effort, you will read it again, stopping to look up each reference.

If and as you do, I'm confident that you will gain a richer appreciation for God and His Word. And so, you will be equipped to understand and handle whatever may transpire. You will be better prepared than ever to trust God and the Lord Jesus Christ in any and every circumstance. You will find that gaining knowledge of His prophetic Word, you will want to purify your every thought and deed [1 John 3:1-3]. "Even so, come, Lord Jesus!"

APPENDIX 1

Day of the Lord

Old Testament Scriptures referring to the **"DAY OF THE LORD"**
[note: shown in the sequence in which each was revealed]

Joel 1:15; 2:1, 11, 31; 3:14
Amos 5:18, 20
Isaiah 2:12; 13:6, 9
Zephaniah 1:7, 14
Jeremiah 46:10
Ezekiel 13:5; 30:3
Obadiah 1:15
Zechariah 14:1
Malachi 4:5

O. T. Scriptures indicating **"in that day"**, and referring to the
DAY OF THE LORD

Deuteronomy 3:17; 31:18
Joel 3:18
Amos 2:16; 8:3, 9, 13
Hosea 1:5; 2:16, 18, 21
Micah 2:4; 4:6; 5:10; 7:11-12
Isaiah 2:11, 17, 20; 3:7, 18; 4:1, 2; 5:30; 7:18, 21, 23; 10:20, 27; 11:10-11; 12:1, 4; 17:4, 7, 9; 19:16, 18-19, 21, 23-24; 22:20, 25; 24:21; 25:9; 26:1; 27:1-2, 12-13; 28:5; 29:18; 30:23; 31:7; 52:6

Zephaniah 3:11, 16
Jeremiah 4:9; 30:8; 39:16-17; 49:22, 26; 50:30
Ezekiel 29:21; 38:19; 39:11
Obadiah 1:8
Haggai 2:23
Zechariah 2:11; 3:10;9:16; 12:3-4, 6, 8-9, 11; 13:1-2, 4

New Testament Scriptures referring to the beginning of the
DAY OF THE LORD

Acts 2:20
James 5:7-8
1 Thessalonians 1:10; 2:16, 19; 3:13; 4:16-17 [initiates the Day of the Lord];
5:2-3, 4, 9, 23
2 Thessalonians 1:7-10
1 Corinthians 3:13; 5:5
Romans 13:12
2 Corinthians 1:14
Ephesians 5:6
Philippians 1:6
Colossians 3:4
1 Timothy 6:14-15
Titus 2:13
1 Peter 1:5; 2:12; 4:7; 5:4
2 Peter 3:10; 12
2 Timothy 1:18; 4:1
Hebrews 9:28; 10:25-26
Jude 14-15
Revelation 3:3, 10

Life in the Millennial Kingdom

DURATION: REVELATION 20:2-7
PEOPLE:

- LIVING, SAVED JEWS [EZEKIEL 20:33ff].
- LIVING, SAVED GENTILES [MATTHEW 25:31ff].
- RESURRECTED O.T. SAINTS [DANIEL 12:1-2].
- ALL WHO ENTER AS LIVING BEINGS ARE SAVED INDIVIDUALS. THEY WILL HAVE CHILDREN AND GRANDCHILDREN, SOME OF WHOM WILL REBEL WHEN SATAN IS LOOSED.

SATAN AND ALL:

- SATAN BOUND IN ABYSS [REV 20:1-3].
- 2 BEASTS IN GEHENNA [REV 19:19-21].

LIFE AND LIVING IN M.K.:

- LONG LIFE [ISAIAH 65:20].
- BEGET CHILDREN [ISAIAH 65:23].
- CORPORAL PUNISHMENT [ISAIAH 65:20]
- BUILD AND PLANT [ISAIAH 65:22].
- PEACE IN NATURE [ISAIAH 11:8-9; 65:24-25].
- PEACE WITH GENTILES [ISAIAH 66:12].
- EGYPT & ASSYRIA [ISAIAH 19:16-25].

- WORSHIP; OFFERINGS [ISAIAH 66:20-22].

CONDITIONS:

- FRUITFUL [ISAIAH 41:18-20].
- RIVERS IN THE DESERT [ISAIAH 43:19-20].
- EDEN-LIKE [ISAIAH 51:3].
- PLENTY, GOOD [ISAIAH 48:9-12].
- PROSPERITY [ISAIAH 54:11-14].
- NATURE IN HARMONY [ISAIAH 55:12-13].
- GLORIOUS LIVING [ISAIAH 30:23-26].
- JUSTICE; PEACE [ISAIAH 32:16-18].
- DESERT BLOSSOMS [ISAIAH 35:1-2].

INDWELT BY HOLY SPIRIT:

- [ISAIAH 32:15 44:3].
- [JEREMIAH 24:7; 31:33, 32:39].
- [EZEKIEL 11:19; 18:31 36:26; 37:14; 39:29].
- [JOEL 2:28-29].
- [ZECHARIAH 12:10].

PRIMACY OF ISRAEL:

- HONORED BY ALL [ISAIAH 49:22-23]
- EXPANDING; HEIRS [ISAIAH 54:3]
- WEALTH FROM OTHERS [ISAIAH 60: 5-15]
- INHERIT THE LAND [ISAIAH 60:21]
- PLANT AND PROSPER [ISAIAH 61:4-9]

APPENDIX 3

Scripture References

REVELATION

LaVergne, TN USA
29 November 2009

165228LV00002BB/3/P